Library of
Davidson College

MILLFIELD ON SATURDAY

Searching for Community in a Metropolitan Village

MATTHEW MELKO
THOMAS E. KOEBERNICK
DAVID MICHAEL ORENSTEIN

Wright State University Press

307.76
M526m

Copyright © 1994 by
Wright State University Press
Wright State University
Dayton, Ohio 45435

All rights reserved
Printed in the United States of America
British Cataloging in Publication Information Available

Distributed by arrangement with
University Publishing Associates,℠ Inc.
4720 Boston Way
Lanham, Maryland 20706

3 Henrietta Street
London WC2E 8LU England

Library of Congress Cataloging-in-Publication Data

Melko, Matthew.
Millfield on Saturday : searching for community in a
  metropolitan village / by Matthew Melko,
  Thomas E. Koebernick, David Michael Orenstein.
        p.   cm.
Includes bibliographical references.
1. Villages—Ohio—Case studies. 2. Community—Case studies.
  3. Social surveys—Ohio. I. Koebernick, Thomas E.
    II. Orenstein, David Michael. III. Title.
HN79.03M45   1994   307.76'2—dc20   93–40796 CIP

ISBN 1–882090–09–8 (cloth : alk. paper)
ISBN 1–882090–10–1 (pbk. : alk. paper)

∞™ The paper used in this publication meets the minimum requirements of
American National Standard for Information Sciences—Permanence
of Paper for Printed Library Materials, ANSI Z39.48–1984.

95-9926

ACY-8659

ACKNOWLEDGMENTS

Our thanks to Freda Kinyon, Lois Walker, Wendell Marshall, Betty Snow, Glena Buchholtz, Jennifer Bayard, Diana Bertke, Lisa Paxton, Lynn Morgan, the woman with the Italian name who typed some of the transcripts, the Wright State Faculty Development Committee, Mary Ridgway, and Bruce Stiver.

A special thanks to all the gracious residents of Millfield who welcomed us into their homes, tolerated our endless questions, and shared with us their Saturday time.

TABLE OF CONTENTS

I. Welcome to Millfield 1
II. Studying Neighborhoods 19
III. The Perception of Community 33
IV. Community Image Versus Urban Activity 41
V. Neighbors and Family 59
VI. Circles of Acquaintance 75
VII. Memories of the Past, Fears of the Future:
     When the City Is at the Gates 111
VIII. Millfield on Saturday 127
Appendix 139
Bibliography 147
Index 151

Chapter I

Welcome to Millfield

Introduction

A central feature of the discipline of sociology since the institutionalization of the field by such figures as Durkheim, Weber, Tönnies, and Park has been a concern with the nature of community in modern industrialized societies. The notion of community is a subtle one because it involves more than just the physical proximity of households. The interactions of individuals living within a shared space, as well as the images (or perceptions) that underlie their interactions, are also fundamental dimensions of our sense of community. The relationship between community images and community actions can be complex and can range from a polar extreme, in which community participants' images are in relative conformity with their actions, to an opposite extreme, in which (at least to the outside observer) dearly held images of community life and actual activity appear to be incongruous.

We have undertaken the present study to better understand the nature of community as it currently exists in our increasingly metropolitan society. Building on more than a century of theory and research, we have developed a series of hypotheses that we will explore and, to some extent, test in a study of a small Midwestern community that, for purposes of this book, we call Millfield. (Millfield and other community names are pseudonyms. The research site is in a metropolitan area of Ohio.) Data for the study were collected by three professional sociologists using open-ended, face-to-face interviews with household members. The analysis of the data is both quantitative and qualitative, with an emphasis on the latter. We view the members of Millfield (and society in general) not as static creatures whose behavior is determined by laws of statistical regularities, but as beings whose images of themselves, friends, family, neighbors, community, and so on influence the actions they formulate and reformulate in relation to one another. Accordingly, we have made a great effort to present the images of community members in their own words and to relate the contexts in which their utterances were made.

All of the interviews were conducted in respondents' homes on Saturday, when we believe community orientations are of greater salience than during the work and school week—hence the title: *Millfield on Saturday*. As much as possible we endeavored to avoid the technical language of the specialist so that our findings will be comprehensible to the educated layperson and useful to the professional social scientist. By concentrating on one community, Millfield, and detailing that community's geographical and social settings, we hope to present a more comprehensive picture of community life than could be achieved from a broader, less-focused sampling.

Setting

Millfield looks like a self-contained community. Located at the edge of the greater Brixton area off Route 69, just before you reach the satellite city of Corinth, and incorporated into suburban Coopertown, it appears very different from Brixton, Corinth, or the rest of Coopertown. Greater Brixton is a medium-sized city surrounded by a considerable suburban area. Houses are made of brick or wood. The city has neighborhoods of different styles, but they aren't strikingly visible to the untutored eye. If you fell asleep on the bus and woke up, you wouldn't know instantly where you were by the style of the side streets.

Like many urban areas, greater Brixton has expanded since World War II. The expanding population of the postwar baby boom, the building of two intersecting interstate highways, and the Federal Housing Authority favoring new housing over renovation have led to a great increase in the suburban population, the building of thousands of ranch-style houses, and the concomitant development of numerous shopping centers in what had been outlying areas.

One of the consequences of this expansion is that autonomous farming villages near Brixton have been surrounded by the suburbs, and the farmland has been sold. Sometimes the village remains the center of town. The oldest and often most charming houses are at the heart of the business district. At other times, as in the case of Millfield, the suburban center is elsewhere and the village becomes a distinctive but nevertheless incidental part of the suburb.

The suburbs sum up what many Americans think of when they hear the phrase "urban sprawl." There are many ranch houses on large lots, so they stand apart from one another in uniform rows, most of them less than four decades old, their areas characterized by green lawns fertilized by local companies with names like Chem-lawn or Beauty Green. The trees grow very slowly and still provide little shade on streets optimistically named Laurel Gardens, Larch Lane, or Catalpa Circle.

Welcome to Millfield

The suburb surrounding Millfield is Coopertown. On a 1955 map, Coopertown was a rural township, Millfield a separate village. Thirty years later the population of Coopertown was more than thirty thousand and Millfield part of its incorporated area. Coopertown is characterized by brick ranch houses on large lots and long streets, so that neighbors can be as distant as they wish and neighborhoods difficult to perceive. Realtors advertise Coopertown as a place where "you can reach out and touch a tree," but you would probably have to walk quite a way if you were susceptible to such a fetish, unless you rode to the tree on your mower.

Coopertown is connected to Brixton and Corinth by Route 69, a four lane, limited access highway. If you are driving on Route 69 from Brixton toward Corinth, you will pass the Cooper Valley Mall, then cross Iron Monger and Millfield Roads. If you continue past Millfield Road you will enter Corinth passing, as one Corinth resident says describing the route to his house, "every fast food restaurant known to man."

But the greater Brixton area is surrounded by farm country, and the urban resident who grows weary of traffic and fast food restaurants can cut off on a two-lane side road and very quickly be passing farms, with occasional houses surrounded by big trees and a nearby cluster of recently painted barns, fields of different colors, Holstein cows, and, when in season, corn and soy beans. The city dweller sometimes looks wistfully at these houses. What kind of life would that be? But the cost! And then the work! Up at five o'clock in the morning. No more steady dependable salary. No more sailing or gardening or football games over the weekend.

Coming from Brixton to Corinth, you find that the Cooper Mall exit is obviously not one of these farm roads. Nor does Iron Monger Road sound promising. But what about hanging a left on Millfield Road? (Figure I-1) Then, what a surprise! Instead of the expected half mile of brick ranches before the road turns country, there is a village! A charming, coherent, white clapboard village. It doesn't just run along the road, either. There are several side streets, so it has dimension. Only one business is visible, an attractive grain mill. The lots are smaller than Coopertown's newer norm, so the houses are more clustered. There is a village post office, with people standing outside chatting.

As you come out the other side, crossing Brixton-Corinth Road and reaching the farm road, you may well think: "Now there's a place to live! Real community and real countryside, farms all around, and the houses might not be too expensive. They aren't so big or so new, and you wouldn't have to buy so much land."

4   Millfield on Saturday: Searching for Community in a Metropolitan Village

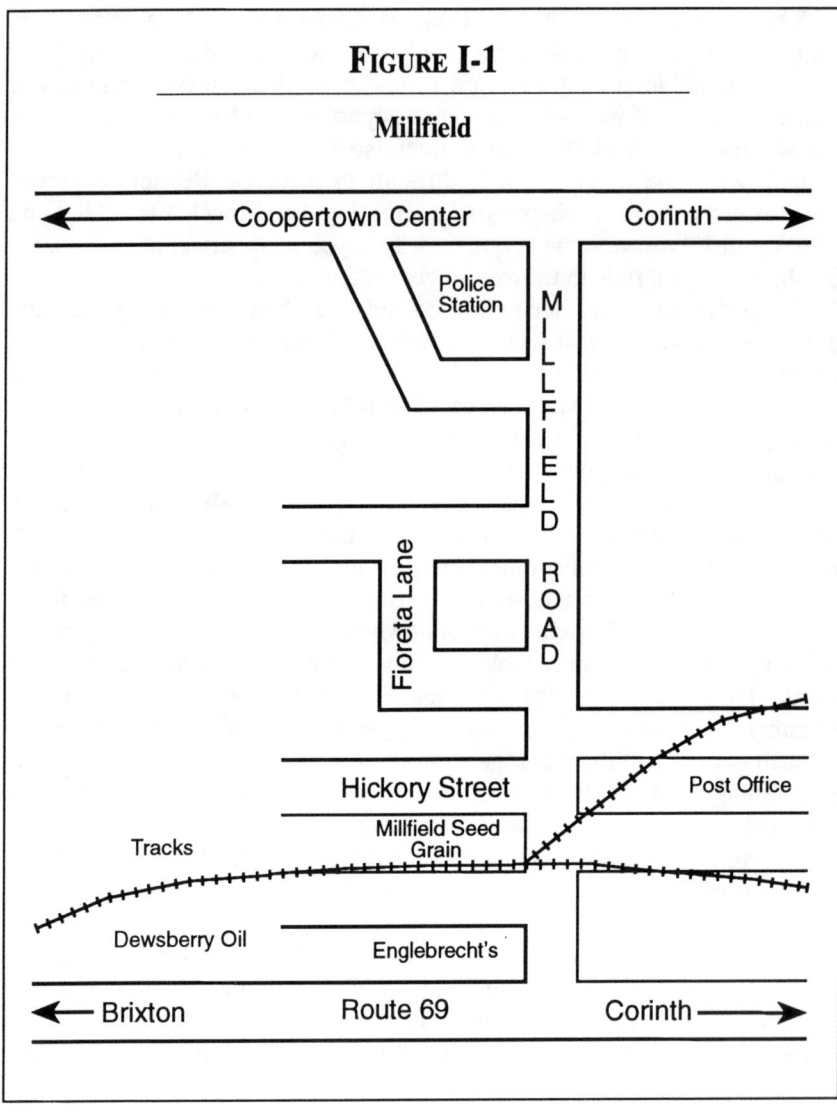

Perception of Community

As one spends more time in Millfield, say interviewing its inhabitants, the charm remains. You can see that the houses are not remarkable, a good many having been built between the World Wars, and they aren't all covered with white clapboard. But they are more clapboard than brick, most of them two-story with front porches, all of them older, from perhaps thirty to eighty years, with one or two going back a century. There is a post office to which almost all residents walk for their mail, a casual atmosphere, cornfields bordering the village, and an absence of sidewalks. There are also a few junked automobiles here and there. But the spell is such that both a research assistant and one of the authors felt a strong desire to live there. Not only would you have a charming community, but you wouldn't have to do any farming, and you'd have the advantages of greater Brixton, with many good paying work possibilities; access to movies, libraries, theaters, clubs, supermarkets, antique shops, department stores, restaurants; and all the other things that urbanites must have.

But then, if we have this feeling driving through or visiting, would not others have it as well? And would not some of them follow through, buy a house, and move to Millfield? But if they did, would they not, as we would, continue with their jobs in greater Brixton, eat at various restaurants on Fridays, buy from the nearby fast foods when too tired to cook, purchase clothes from Sears or Lazarus, and continue weekends with whatever hobbies?

Could it be, then, that this enclave is largely inhabited by urbanites who have a nostalgia for community? If so, have they largely undercut their objective by creating something else? It would seem unlikely that a village at the edge of an urban area would bear much resemblance to the inhabitants of Vidich and Bensman's Springdale (1985), for that village played a more important part in the lives of its inhabitants than any other locality. But the inhabitants of Millfield, one might guess, liked the village well enough, but lived much of their lives in the urban area surrounding it. We might have called them *urban villagers* if the term had not already been appropriated by Herbert Gans (1962).

Gans' urban villagers, of course, had a good claim to be villagers. The area they lived in was a village because of its focus, because its inhabitants did spend their lives where they lived, buying, trading, interacting, playing, supporting, dying. Their village was truly a home within the larger city.

Gans' villagers lost their home to urban renewal. In recent years, other such villagers have lost their homes to the gentrifiers, the wealthy middle-class members who have returned from the suburb to the city, buying potentially beautiful but rundown Victorian houses and, at considerable expense and energy, restoring them.

Though the middle-class gentrifier may not be welcomed by the urban villager, there are some similarities between the two. Gentrifiers love the neighborhood and enjoy the city. They put great energy, enthusiasm, and expense into the renovation of their homes, and when they go outside their community, it is usually to the adjacent downtown area, not to the suburban mall. Their clash with the urban villager is often accidental. They may not intend to drive the villager out, and they might even prefer a mixed neighborhood. But inevitably their purchasing power raises rents, and their improvements raise taxes. The villager is forced to leave for poorer, more remote housing and for a struggle to restore community.

Is there a corresponding conflict in Millfield? Does the middle-class entrant drive up the price of housing? If that were so, there still might not be the conflict that has occurred in the urban village, for if the price of housing goes up, taxes would not necessarily follow, since there would be less drive for home improvement. Whereas gentrifiers see possibilities in a Victorian shell, immigrants to Millfield would be purchasing a thirty- to eighty-year-old house, ready to live in. They would not have to invest the cost of their houses in repairs. Moreover, those who live there may remain. If they do move, it may be because the offering prices for houses are high.

We might suspect, then, that immigrants to Millfield would be content to be villagers without seeking gentry status. They would be attracted by the image of community—the beauty, the coziness that provides an enclave of peace at the edge of the lively but enervating urban area. Perhaps the immigrant buys a home from a rural resident who sees Millfield somewhat differently, as the place where he or she grew up, as the place where family lives, perhaps as a place a little outmoded in comparison with the ranch houses with big lawns that characterize the rest of Coopertown and most of the greater Brixton suburbs. Do urban immigrants perhaps find solace in walking to the post office to pick up their mail and greeting some rural neighbors, neighbors who perhaps feel their mail ought to be delivered to their mailboxes, as it is in the rest of Coopertown? Does the immigrant take a dim view of the junked automobile that undermines the beauty of the community, a car perhaps owned by a native neighbor who staunchly believes that each individual has the right to do what he or she wishes with personal property?

One hypothesis, then, might be that there would be a different sense of community between the native villager, who has lived and grown up in Millfield or surrounding Coopertown, and the urban immigrant, who moves in from greater Brixton or another part of the country and chooses Millfield as a place to live precisely because it appears to be a community, not merely a collection of ranch-style houses.

Images of Millfield

After spending a couple of Saturdays in Millfield, one accumulates a large quantity of images, myths, and symbols that seem to be community property. Some are widely shared, some narrowly but vividly held. Some can be visually inferred. What follows are the images, myths, and symbols that we most remember. Along the way we shall try to test the validity of many of them. But however valid they may prove to be by empirical investigation, they were themselves factors—some more important than others—in shaping the image of Millfield.

Community. Millfield is a community. This is visually apparent and almost universally accepted by residents. If the sociological definitions of community don't fit Millfield, the sociological definitions will have to be re-examined.

Cluster. The image is of a cluster of houses, not a row. The irregular way in which the houses were built, the curvature of the lanes, all add to the impression of community.

Post Office. People walk to the post office, greeting neighbors on the way. Everyone meets there, talks, and gets the latest gossip.

Everybody Knows Everybody. Strangers are instantly recognizable because Millfielders all know one another by sight if not by name.

Walking. Millfield is small enough that you walk from place to place. You get in your car only if you are going somewhere else. No one would ever drive to the post office.

Front Porches. People sit out on them and watch other Millfielders pass by. Walking Millfielders call out to people sitting on porches or stroll over to chat.

Friendliness. Millfield is a friendly community. People are pleasant and supportive to one another.

Charm. Millfield has inherent charm. You want to take pictures. Individual houses are not remarkable, but, collectively, they and the atmosphere in general are seductive.

Clapboard. Unlike most houses in Coopertown, the majority of houses in Millfield are covered by clapboard. They are less utilitarian and have to be painted from time to time, but it is the clapboard, taken with the cluster and the walking, that gives Millfield its charm.

Mill. No longer in use, it is still a symbol of an earlier period and the landmark of the village.

Cornfields. Another symbol, this time of a rural life. Cornfields are restful and to be protected against the incursion of the dreaded condominium. When the corn grows up, the village is safely surrounded, symbolically protected.

Close to Nature. Though corn isn't exactly natural, it provides a rural background against the impending city, a haven for birds and animals not seen in the city, restful night sounds, peaceful dawns.

Family. A great place to raise a family. Families are happier in Millfield, closer together.

Working on Houses. On Saturday you'll find Millfielders working on their houses, replacing double pane windows with six-over-six sash windows, painting in flat, colonial colors, removing garish gewgaws, improving the water supply, and replacing roof gutters.

Neighborly Help. When they work on their houses and cars, they can expect help and advice from their neighbors, who lend tools and labor cheerfully, often without being asked.

Trust. The people trust one another. You can leave doors unlocked, valuables in your car or on the porch, or a cigar box to put money in at an unattended garage sale.

Safety. It is a safe place to live because strangers are recognized, because everyone walks, because everyone knows everyone. And unlike many houses in Coopertown, most of those in Millfield have cellars for refuge against tornadoes.

Neighborhood Watch. But the other side of that is that strangers are noticed and reported; sociologists administering questionnaires had better check in with the police, who will get a dozen inquiries during the day, especially about Eastern-type sociologists with beards.

Junk. While strangers may be viewed with concern, junk is okay. If you want to have six old cars in your yard, that's your business. But there is a suspicion that those who are working on houses may not be enthusiastic about a neighbor's junk.

Ducks. If the first article in the Millfield Bill of Rights gives one the right to junk, the second gives the right to own ducks. You don't have to have a permit to raise ducks, and your ducks may roam freely, certain that they will be greeted in a friendly fashion by neighbors.

Image Versus Activity

By its appearance, Millfield would seem to be a farm village of considerable charm, the kind of place where everybody knows everybody, where everybody pitches in to gather the crop before gathering for the Harvest Ball. But further observation shows it can't be that. As we have seen, this charming village of older clapboard houses is incorporated into Coopertown, a town of widely spaced ranch houses. And Coopertown, in turn, is part of greater Brixton, an area of nearly a million people. Millfield, therefore, though clearly a distinct entity, is not an isolated country town, but an urban enclave. It does retain its visual autonomy, its clustered older houses contrasting sharply with the Coopertown ranches. This autonomy is reinforced by Millfield signs at each end of Millfield Road, the two main entrances to the village.

But the village is not economically autonomous. It does not contain the amenities you would expect to find in an autonomous village: no country store, no gas station. Millfield Feed and Grain, the dominant architectural structure in the village, is not an active business. There is a body shop, a post office, and a police station that, it turns out, is a branch station for other parts of Coopertown as well as Millfield. There is farmland surrounding the village, but the sixty households of the village could not be supported by that farmland. It must be, therefore, that most of the inhabitants work outside Millfield, unless there are home businesses that do not require local visibility.

It becomes apparent, then, that while Millfield once stood by itself, Brixton to the west and Corinth to the east have gradually expanded until the village has been surrounded, without losing its visual coherence. So who lives in Millfield? Are these the sons and daughters of farmers now working in factories or as waitresses and store clerks? Or are they accountants and lawyers, or perhaps military personnel from the nearby base, who want the advantages of country atmosphere with access to good paying work, movies, libraries, theaters, clubs, supermarkets, antique shops, department stores, restaurants, and all the other things that urbanites require?

How important is community to most Millfielders? Are they in fact commuters, heading every day to work in Brixton or Corinth along Route 69? Do they find solace in the gentle beauty of Millfield, without feeling an obligation to support the community? Do they enjoy walking to the post office on Saturday to pick up the mail, recognizing neighbors by face, perhaps knowing their first names, but without deep involvement in the life of the community? For if they are commuters, the main part of their lives during the week would be in the greater Brixton area, not Millfield.

On Saturday, will they then be occupied with Millfield affairs, or will their lives be diffused through greater Brixton? Do they socialize with their neighbors or with friends and kinsmen from all over the city? Do they garden in Millfield, or play golf on one of the greater Brixton golf links? And what of their spouses? If they are also working, we would expect the lives of husbands and wives to be similar. If not, if the wife is at home, where will her energies be? Is her social involvement in Millfield or in the Coopertown school system, the greater Brixton League of Women Voters, or a church more likely to be in Coopertown or Corinth? And the children: if they go to Coopertown schools, won't their friends more likely live in other areas of Coopertown?

Our expectation, then, was that Millfield would be neither village nor urban community. It would be a pleasant place to live for people whose lives were diffused through greater Brixton. In some respects, however, it could resemble a gentrifying area of the inner city. But the people moving in are not racially or economically distinguishable from those who live there, and perhaps on weekends they even adopt the villagers' dress, overalls rather than jeans. Nor would the owner-renter distinction be as strongly drawn as it would be in a gentrifying community, nor are the houses in obvious need of repair. In appearance they are already acceptably middle class.

It therefore seemed likely that most people living in Millfield would perceive it to be a friendly, neighborly place, with a great deal of social interaction going on. They would also see it as a haven of peace and seclusion from city bustle. But in fact their busy lives, both on weekdays and weekends, would keep them from either socializing or experiencing much of the tranquility the village seemed to offer. And as for the image that everybody knows everybody, we take that to mean that at the post office one would usually recognize a stranger or a visitor, but not be on a first name basis or know where everyone lives.

Past and Future

If Millfield is not the farm village it appears to be, surely it has experienced a great deal of change in the past three decades. To what extent can it have remained a quiet village community with the city at the gates? Has a vast internal social change taken place? Are the residents aware of the change? Do they fear further change in the future?

What seemed likely? To begin with, it seemed likely that people who live in Millfield must be aware of the apparent peaceful community atmosphere. And they must strongly want to maintain it. They are very aware of changes that have taken place in the past, but do not expect change in the future. And thus we wouldn't be surprised if long-time residents had a sense of the good old days, a feeling that things were better in the past than they are now.

It seemed likely that other urban people would react as the visiting sociologists did. What a neat place to live! Therefore, some of the houses may have been bought by people working in greater Brixton who were attracted by this vestige of apparent community in a sea of opulent but anonymous ranch houses. Yet, there would be other residents who had lived there longer, who bought when housing was cheaper, or who inherited their houses. Would there be any conflict between them about how Millfield is or should be? We thought there might. There would probably be some agreement that Millfield should be maintained. But wouldn't the people moving in, with better educations and urban backgrounds, want to keep the village as it is, but beautifully restored? The rural people, on the other hand, while they would want it kept as it is, would not be concerned about restoration and would want freedom to continue doing whatever they like to do, regardless of how that might affect the appearance of the village. Further, these rural, less-educated dwellers might be more willing to accept urban improvements such as streetlights, sidewalks, and home-delivered mail. The urbanites would want to forego these improvements or even resist them in order to keep the village a village.

We thought there might be a difference in perceptions of history. The urban-educated would be likely to have a more complete set of information about Millfield than the rural people. Millfield has a long history for an Ohio community, going back to the early nineteenth century. It had been the first county seat and was once a transportation center and a locus for manufacturing and agriculture. Long-time residents, on the other hand, might have more information about past activities, with less concern about their historical significance. And, of course, they would have more anecdotal history.

We thought all residents would be more likely to perceive change in symbols and things than in people, because these were more visible when considering change and because of a shared desire that the village really not change. And we also expected that the expansion of Brixton and the incorporation of Millfield into Coopertown must have more of an effect than is visible. We expected that all residents were likely to fear building and development near Millfield, with a resultant disappearance of cornfields, increase in traffic, and other changes that would undermine village tranquility.

The incorporation had occurred only two years prior to our study. So, in a sense, Millfield is now a neighborhood, but a neighborhood with a 180-year history as a distinct community. The incorporation was largely defensive, to stave off annexation efforts on the part of Brixton itself. But incorporation could mean changes that have to do with the problems of Coopertown. Will there be sidewalks? Mail delivery? Electric street lights? Some may hope so. Some may fear so. But we did not expect these apprehensions really to be deep. We thought that people might expect to leave Millfield, if at all, because a change in jobs forced them to move elsewhere or because their children grew up and their houses were too big to maintain. We did not expect that they would really be worried about being forced to move by some external catastrophic change, such as the bulldozing of Millfield to make another mall.

Some Preliminary Hypotheses

After we had seen Millfield, but before we studied it, one of the authors jotted down some hypotheses to be considered in composing a survey. Most of these have already been referred to. They may be worth keeping in mind as we explore some of the social relations in the village.

1. Social networks (i.e., friendships, family activity, social organization involvement) are stronger for most people in the greater Brixton-Corinth area than they are in Millfield.
2. The majority of Millfielders are immigrants from some other Ohio community.
3. The primary reason for buying a home in Millfield is because of its charm.
4. Millfield is favored as a place to live more by women than by men.
5. Those who promote Millfield as a community are mostly women.
6. If nearness to work were the first criterion for choice of a place to live, most Millfielders would be living somewhere else.
7. The immigrants are bigger Millfield boosters than the natives.
8. Long-time Millfield residents remember more community activity twenty-five and fifty years ago than they perceive today.
9. Family relationships are as strong today as they were twenty-five years ago.
10. Divorce in Millfield is average when compared to greater Brixton, both among long-time residents and short-time residents.
11. Kinship relations are similar for Millfield short-time residents and long-time residents.
12. Even though community is not really important to them, Millfielders like living there and would move only if a job change forced them to do so.
13. Millfielders perceive that others in the village have closer community relations than they do themselves.
14. Friday activities concern work or household, not community. Saturday activities concern household, kin, and outside Millfield activity, not community.

Welcome to Millfield 13

TABLE I-1

Millfield Sample

Household Number	Years of Education	Grammar	Work or School	Age	Years in Millfield	Previous Years	Previous Residence	Gender	Relationship	Interviewed	Own Home?	Marital Status
1	12	C	R Road Supt.	67	62	No	Ohio Village	M	Father	Y	Y	M
	16	T	Machinist	30	30	No	None	M	Son	Y		N
4		T	Electronics Tech.					M			Y	M
			Secretary					F		Y		M
			Student		1							
6	12	T	Wholesale Grocer	65	36	No	Ohio Town	M	Husband	Y	Y	M
	14		Secretary	61	36	No	Ohio Town	F	Wife	N		M
	14+		OSU	22	22	No	None	M	Son	N		N
8	12	C	Does Work	46	5	No	Coopertown	F	Wife	Y	Y	M
			R	25	5	No	Coopertown	M	Husband	N		M
			Works for Dept.		5	No	Coopertown	M	Son	N		N
			of Education	20	5	No	Coopertown	M	Son	N		N
10	8	C	R Grocer,	52	23	No	Brixton Suburb	M	Husband	Y	Y	M
	12	C	Landscape, Painting	50	23	No	Brixton Suburb	F	Wife	Y		M
			Bank Teller									
12	16+	T	Air Force Capt.,	28	1	No	Texas City	F	Wife	Y	Y	M
	12	T	BAFB	49	0	No	Texas City	F	Mother	Y		
	8+	C	No	14	0	No	Texas City	F	Sister	Y		N
			High School									
14	12	C	Foreman, BPL	45	14	No	Corinth	M	Husband	Y	Y	M
	12		Fabric Manager	39	14	No	Corinth	F	Wife	N		M
	14		BSU	20	14	No	Corinth	M	Son	N		N
	12		BSU	18	14	No	Corinth	M	Son	N	N	N
	9		High School	15	14	No	Corinth	M	Son	N		N
15	14	T	Mechanic, BPL	32	2	No	Coopertown	M		Y	Y	N

TABLE I-1 (CONTINUED)
Millfield Sample

Household Number	Years of Education	Grammar	Work or School	Age	Years in Millfield	Previous Years	Previous Residence	Gender	Relationship	Interviewed	Own Home?	Marital Status
20	15	T	No	26	2	1	Coopertown	F	Wife	N	N	M
	15		Materials Science	24	2	1	Coopertown	M	Husband	N		M
	0		BSU	4	2							N
	0		Preschool	2	2	No	Coopertown	F	Sibling	N		N
	0		Preschool	0	0	No	None		Daughter	N		N
	0		Preschool			No	None		Sibling	N		N
24	10	C	R Postal Clerk	69	23	No	Brixton Suburb	F	Wife	Y	Y	M
	10		Truck Driver	58	23	No	Brixton Suburb	M	Husband	N		M
25	16+	T	R Aeronautical Engr. and Farming	49	14	No	Michigan	M	Husband	Y	Y	M
	16		No	49	14	No	SE Asia	F	Wife	N		M
	7		School	13	13	No	None	M	Son	N		N
	12+	T	BSU	22	14	No	Michigan	F	Daughter	N		N
	12+		BSU	21	14	No	Michigan	M	Son	N		N
26	13	C	R Liquor Salesman	66	2	No	Brixton Suburb	M	Husband	Y	Y	M
	12	C	R Account Clerk	67	67	No	None	F	Wife	Y	Y	M
29	16+	T	H.S. Principal	41	15	No	Corinth	M	Husband	Y	Y	M
	16		Preschool Teacher	42	15	11	Corinth	F	Wife	Y		M
	11		School	17	15	No	Corinth	M	Son	N		N
	9		School	15	15	No	None	M	Son	N		N
	11		School	6	6	No	None	M	Son	N		N
35		C	No	75	54	No	Coopertown	F		Y	Y	M
38	16+	T	Physicist, BAFB	36	8	No	Brixton	M	Husband	Y	Y	M
	15	T	Accountant	33	8	No	Brixton	F	Wife	Y		M
			School			No	None	F	Daughter	N		N
			Preschool	1	1	No	None		Sibling	N		N
40	16	T	R Systems Analyst, Real Estate	42	10	No	Brixton Suburb	M	Husband	Y	Y	M
	16	T	None	41	10	No	Brixton Suburb	F	Wife	Y		M

TABLE I-1 (CONTINUED)
Millfield Sample

Household Number	Years of Education	Grammar	Work or School	Age	Years in Millfield	Previous Years	Previous Residence	Gender	Relationship	Interviewed	Own Home?	Marital Status
41	16+ 15 0	T T —	CPA None	30 24 0	3 3 0	No No No	Brixton Brixton Suburb None	M F M	Husband Wife Son	Y Y N	Y	M M N
42	12	C	Sanitary Inspector City Engineer	35	7	No No	Ohio City	M F	Son Mother	Y Y	Y	N
46	12 13	C C	R. Cafeteria Toolmaker	67 6x	67 36	No No	None Ohio Town	F M	Wife Husband	Y Y	Y	M M
48	12 16 13 15 11	T R T T	Svc. man, BPL Lib. Tech. BAFB BCC BSU Conf. Cen. High School	61 58 22 21 17	19 19 19 19 17	No No No No No	Brixton Suburb Brixton Suburb Brixton Suburb Brixton Suburb None	M F M M F	Husband Wife Son Son Daughter	Y Y Y N Y	Y	M M N N N
49	8 11 12	C C C	R. Shop Owner No Yes	66 64 20	55 64 20	No No No	Ohio Town None None	M F M	Husband Wife Son	Y Y Y	Y	M M N
51	10 12 9 4	C C 	School Employ. Avon Sales Lady School School	39 34 15 10	9 9 9 9	26 1 No No	Corinth Corinth Corinth Corinth	M F F M	Husband Wife Daughter Son	Y Y Y N	Y	M M N N
56	12 10	T	Motel Maid Mechanic	36 47	2 2	No No	Ohio Town Ohio Town	F M	Wife Husband	Y N	Y	M M
59	10 14+ 9	C	School employ. BAFB School	45 46 15	18 18 15	No No No	Lincoln None None	M F M	Wife Husband Son	Y N N	Y	M M N

KEY

C = Colloquial
T = Textbook
R = Retired
Household Number: Each household was assigned a number, whether interviewed or not.

OSU = Ohio State University BSU = Brixton State University
BAFB = Brixton Airforce Base BCC = Brixton Community College
BPL = Brixton Power and Light

Y = Yes M = Married
N = No N = Never Married

Reflections on Method

To test these and other hypotheses about Millfield, we administered a fifty-five-item, open-ended questionnaire (see Appendix) to an area-stratified sample of twenty-four households, comprising about 40 percent of the occupied houses in Millfield. Of the sixty-three household members of school age or older, we caught forty-one at home, about two-thirds. (For a more detailed breakdown of the sample, see Table I-1.) Our intention was to interview the residents of these households on a single Saturday, but people being away from home and the very hospitality of the Millfielders made it impossible to complete the interviews in one day. So we had to go back on a second and, in a few cases, even on a third Saturday. In any event, all interviews were conducted on Saturdays of the same month (October), all beautiful fall days when a variety of activities would be possible. For the most part our sample was random, except that we did interview two or three people for special reasons, such as seniority or leadership in promoting the community. This led to some problems, because word soon got around that sociologists with tape recorders were doing interviews, and the most hospitable were apt to call us over to interview them. We had to refuse if they were not in the sample while seeking out those who were reluctant or not available until the following week.

We interviewed households rather than individuals. That meant sometimes a family sitting around the dining room table, sometimes the only person who happened to be home. It also meant that sometimes an additional person, arriving from somewhere or other, would join us in mid-interview.

There are limitations in every method. The decision to interview households rather than individuals seems appropriate for a community study, since attitudes are likely to be shared. If one person says he came to Millfield because of the community and the other person does not, we can't be sure that the other person agrees. So generally we let whoever responded answer, then asked if others had anything to add. Table I-1 contains an inventory of the households interviewed, who was at home and who wasn't, ages, gender, years of schooling, relationships, grammar, years of residence, and other information about each household resident. Of the twenty-four families interviewed, twenty-three owned their homes. One or more members of fourteen of these families had lived in Millfield for ten years or more. The mean and median residence of the longest resident in a household was twenty-three years.

Considering that twenty-one of the twenty-four households were owned or rented by married people, the population composition summarized in Table I-2 was surprisingly male (55.1 percent male, 39.1 percent female, and 5.8 percent unknown). This was partly because the children under nineteen

TABLE I-2

Composition of Population Among Interviewed Households

Age	Male	Female	Unknown	Total	Percent
0–9	5	1	3	6	8.7
10–19	7	3		10	14.5
20–29	9	4		13	18.8
30–39	6	4		10	14.5
40–49	7	6		10	14.5
50–59	2	2		4	5.8
60–69	6	5		11	15.9
70–79	0	1		1	1.4
Unknown	2	1	1	4	5.8
Total	38	27	4	69	
Percent	55.1	39.1	5.8		100

were predominantly male by a 3:1 ratio, which would seem to be purely coincidence. There were also nine sons and only one daughter in the twenty to thirty age category still living with parents.

While a 40 percent sample would seem to be more than adequate to reflect the views of the village, twenty-four households is a small number for quantitative assessments. So we shall refer to numbers and percentages (in a situation in which six households represent 25 percent), but rely more upon qualitative assessments, supported by the actual statements made. The margin for interpretation is wider than one would get from a computerized, longer questionnaire with more quantifiable shorter answers. In Edward G. Hall's terms (1976), this is a high context study, in which nuances mean a great deal and in which interpretations are made in terms of the total body of information provided. Because of the importance of nuance, we shall often use direct quotations because, as you will see, the Millfielder's way of putting a matter sometimes cannot be summarized, corrected, or presented in any other way without becoming something else. For this reason, too, you may sometimes encounter quotations repeated in other contexts, because in these other contexts the same words can have amazingly different meaning. We are limited, also, by the medium in which we are working. You cannot see the tone that occasionally transforms what appears to be innocuous or, in one or two instances, renders innocuous what appears to be pejorative. Millfielders using colloquial language are often careful, balancing "on the one hand" with "on the other hand," and concluding with a hint of concern: "D'ya see what I'm sayin'?"

In an era of sophisticated computer analysis of discrete variables, this approach may seem arcane, even quaint. But we think that the availability of new methods does not preclude continued cross-checking and exploration with old methods. And we hope we have learned from our anthropological colleagues that even methods are cultural. If you are permitted only to answer the question asked and never to provide contexts, you may get nothing but the truth, but you will never approach the whole truth.

Before attempting to answer some of the questions raised, we will consider relevant findings of previous community studies. That task could provide a book in itself, but we have attempted to sort out some of the previous studies that indicate areas of controversy or agreement that may help us formulate and refine questions about Millfield. Is Millfield a genuine community and, as such, a distinctive neighborhood within the larger municipality of Coopertown? As a discrete place with a long history of autonomous village life, is Millfield a holistic social world, one single, undifferentiated communal association? Or within its limited but precise borders, do residents make spatial distinctions regarding social relationships and public identities? Are there neighborhoods within Millfield itself? The notion of the neighborhood as an urban village arose out of observations of how migrants to cities sometimes transformed their areas of residence into relatively homogeneous social worlds based upon a common ethnic subculture. Neighborhoods are turned into urban villages (i.e., culturally self-contained communities). Millfield, on the other hand, presents a different situation in which a village through annexation becomes an urban neighborhood. Chapter II explores the meaning of neighborhood within the context of a community level of social organization.

CHAPTER II

Studying Neighborhoods

"Everybody knows everybody in Millfield." Do they? When they meet at the post office, perhaps each smiles and nods to each. Or most do. Most of the time. But do they know one another? Would they know one another better in the houses in the immediate vicinity or on the same street? Does a small, village-like community such as Millfield still contain spatially distinct social areas that are recognized as separate neighborhoods by its residents? Or is the Millfield community one big neighborhood within the larger Coopertown community?

This chapter explores the meaning of community and neighborhood as defined by urban scholars. Since the late nineteenth century there have been efforts to explain how the Industrial Revolution and the rapid urbanization that accompanied it have changed the social life of those communities affected by it. How do urban communities differ from their rural counterparts? Why have neighborhoods been regarded as important social areas of urban life? What makes a particular area a neighborhood and what does it mean to be a neighbor? Lastly, if Millfield is in some sense a particular neighborhood within the city of Coopertown, then what kind of neighborhood is it? Two models of urban neighborhoods are discussed, the *urban village* and the *community of limited liability*. Which best describes Millfield? In many ways this issue affects the hypotheses raised in Chapter I.

The Urban Community

There has been an ongoing debate among urban scholars as to the nature of the urban neighborhood and the role the neighborhood plays in the social life of urban communities. The sheer number of persons residing in an urban community makes the likelihood very slight of a unified, holistic form of community common in small, rural villages of preindustrial societies. In the modern, industrial society, cities display a great deal of social diversity and competition among various segments of the community. In the past it has been assumed that the scale of city life made it impossible for urban residents to participate meaningfully in a social life that encompassed the totality of a population. Practical constraints limited the mobility of urban residents in the nineteenth century, requiring that most daily activities be carried out within a relatively limited spatial area. Walking being the principal means of transport for the nineteenth century urbanite, activities such as work, worship, shopping, and recreation needed to be located within a mile or two of one's residence. Furthermore, the tremendous growth in urban populations in early industrial cities was due to large numbers of migrants entering cities from a diversity of rural regions and foreign countries. Preference for living around those with similar cultural backgrounds and discrimination by more advantaged social groups in the community encouraged social homogeneity in residential areas. Heightened social divisions based in the new industrial cities, based upon social class, also created economic homogeneity in residential areas tied to the cost of housing.

The existence of residential clusters arising from cultural and regional origins and shared economic status, combined with the presence of a wide range of institutional services and activities used by residents of an area on a regular basis to support their way of life, characterizes the urban neighborhood of early urban researchers. In attempting to understand the impact of the modern city upon the social life of its inhabitants, sociologists have, not surprisingly, focused their studies on the neighborhood. For it was in the neighborhood—that is, among those with whom one lived on a daily basis and participated in a common institutional life—that the quality and form of urban community life could best be observed.

Effrat (1974) points out that the study of urban neighborhoods has largely served to test broader theories of community, namely, the extent to which the traditional modes of community associated with rural village life persist or are lost due to urbanization. The nineteenth century urban neighborhood was regarded as a structural equivalent of the village, the issue being whether the social relations of urban neighbors manifested the same quality of community as their rural predecessors. As early as 1887, the German sociologist, Ferdinand Tönnies, declared the inevitable demise of community in an increasingly industrialized urban society. He saw rural life as a social arrangement that involved intimate, private, and exclusive living together. "In a *Gemeinschaft* the individual is socially immersed as a segment of a social unity, a component of the whole—with that whole being the group." (Flanagan, 1990: 42) "In contrast, *Gessellschaft* is transitory and superficial." (Tönnies, 1887, 1957: 35)

The city, according to Tönnies, heightened class conflict, creating tensions between the interests of capital and labor. Hostility between social groups and the diminished role of family life resulted in human action no longer arising from a will and spirit of unity based upon family and community ties. Instead, life in the city is built around *Gessellschaft* social relationships in which one's actions are calculated based upon the exchange value of the transaction. "Everybody is by himself and isolated, and there exists a condition of tension against all others." (Tönnies, 1887, 1957: 64)

By the middle of the twentieth century, one scholar of community was willing to proclaim the "eclipse of community" in advanced industrial countries such as the United States (Stein, 1960). Louis Wirth (1938), one of the most influential urban sociologists of this century, had already provided a powerful theoretical argument as to why the kind of intense interpersonal relationships Tönnies regarded as the essence of true community (i.e., *Gemeinschaft*) were almost impossible to sustain in the modern city. Its large population (i.e., size) was distributed over a relatively small area (i.e., high density) and included people with a wide diversity of lifestyles, cultural backgrounds, and social positions (i.e., social heterogeneity). Lacking common values and sense of purpose, the urbanite was likely to experience feelings of anomie and alienation, which weakened social conformity and encouraged deviant behaviors. Thus, in the city, one could observe both personal and social disorganization and their harmful results (e.g., crime, social conflict, isolation, and neglect).

While Tönnies and Wirth were writing of the city as a total social system, tests of their theories were mainly carried out through research at the neighborhood level. Over the years these studies have yielded several important generalizations about neighborhoods. One is that neighborhoods are not the only spatially defined social system in urban communities. We also know that the extent of social organization that actually exists at the neighborhood level varies greatly and that such organization often functions differently from what residents may believe. We have also come to regard a community as something more than just the sum of its individual neighborhoods. That is, the extent to which community-like social relationships exist in a given place cannot be determined by understanding the nature of neighborhood social life alone.

Two Models of Community

At present those who study neighborhood life use or address one of two theoretical models in their research. Janowitz (1951) introduced the term *community of limited liability* to describe the then emerging suburban lifestyle. The concept addresses the rather limited importance of the residential neighborhood and even the larger, local community, as a primary focus of social involvement and personal identity. This viewpoint derives from the Wirthian hypotheses noted above. Others have found the existence of the urban village neighborhood, which is noted for its resemblance to Tönnies' *Gemeinschaft* rural village. (cf. Nisbet, 1962; Gusfield, 1975; Banfield, 1968; Gans, 1962; Powell, 1972; Caplan and Killilea, 1976).

To some extent, the *Gesellschaft*-like Wirthian model may have been based upon urban immigrant settlements in the United States when compared with European village life. The subsequent finding of *Gemeinschaft* elements within urban ethnic settlements may reflect the experiences of second generation Americans who did not share the older European village images (Jones, 1904; Woolston, 1909; Pratt, 1911; Woolston, 1938; Olson, 1982).

Using the *Gemeinschaft* model, researchers have discovered an urban village in which family and kinship ties play an important role in binding residents to the neighborhood through shared space and intensive interaction. The extended family is anchored in the neighborhood and supports it in urban villages such as London's Bethnal Manor (Bott, 1960), North Boston (Gans, 1962), or the Addams area in Chicago (Suttles, 1968). The term *urban village* is used because similar binding relationships are found in rural villages (Vidich and Bensman, 1958).

Family life also is important in the community of limited liability, but it is the "isolated nuclear families" rather than extended kinship relations that dominate. The neighborhood becomes less an area of action than a launching pad for social activities in the larger community. Neighborhood involvement centers around family tasks, especially childrearing. Participation is segregated by life-cycle and social roles. Physical separation from extended family is the norm and if kin are available they are likely to be outside the neighborhood. Thus some researchers note the opposing tendencies of interaction with kin and neighboring, especially among the lower classes.

So these two models, the urban village and the community of limited liability, posit two distinct family styles with two contradictory consequences for the communal character of neighborhoods. Such characteristics are probabilities. We are talking more or less, not either-or. When we focus upon a real life neighborhood, like Millfield, there is no guarantee that it can be neatly placed into any ideal type. It may look like a village. People living in it may think of it as a village. But on a given day, a Saturday for instance, their activities may suggest considerable concern with greater Brixton. The serene community may be seen, contradictory though the metaphor may seem, as a launching pad. The assertion that contradictory characteristics can apparently coexist at the same level is not profound; indeed it has been recognized by some of the very researchers responsible for the competing models.

Empirical studies of the past two decades have been approaching these contradictions in various ways. They have relied upon comparative distributions of "communal characteristics" found in various neighborhoods or groups of residents. Multivariant statistical techniques have factored and partialled direct and indirect effects of endogenous and exogenous variables producing statistically significant contributions to the explanation of variance. In other words, they have used contemporary research methods in an attempt to sort out the degree to which people in geographically defined communities or neighborhoods relate to others within those neighborhoods as compared to relating with others outside.

For instance, Albert Hunter's 1975 restudy of a Rochester, New York, neighborhood twenty-five years after the original by Donald Foley (1952) focused on residents' use of local facilities, informal neighboring, and sense of community. The only significant change was a reduction in the use of local facilities. Hunter refers to the persistence of sense of community despite decline of local usage as a limited "ideological community" drawing on Karl Mannheim's distinction between utopia and ideology. Utopian thinking rejects the status quo and the social reality it represents (Mannheim, 1964: 193). He refers to ideology as "the unconscious situational motivation of group thinking." (1964: 39) Ideological thought represents the taken-for-granted reality shared by the members of a particular social group. The neighborhood is seen as an ecological niche for a certain type of urban resident based partly upon location and partly upon ideology. Though people are involved in the life of the city and have work and friends outside the neighborhood, they still perceive shared values within the neighborhood. That perception becomes a factor in choosing to live there. Formal organizational involvement combined with informal neighboring encourages neighborhood solidarity and a sense of community among residents.

Meanwhile, in England, John Kasarda and Morris Janowitz (1974) found that length of residence had a major effect on community attitudes and sentiments, as well as on social bonds, including number of relatives, friends, and acquaintances. They also found that participation in informal organizations fosters more extensive primary contacts in the local community.

More recently, Guest and Lee (1983) compared twenty areas of metropolitan Seattle along nine measures of community attachment. A factor analysis identified both a "village" and a "limited liability" form of social organization. Guest and Lee conclude that "the two types of areas are not well differentiated by neighborhood definitions that reflect a sense of community or institutions."

These studies try to sort out whether or not neighborhoods fit the Park and

Burgess image of places in which residents shop in familiar stores, greet each other as they pass on the street, lend each other assistance, visit on front porches, and gather in taverns or churches to discuss local issues (Park and Burgess, 1925; Olson, 1982).

Who Is My Neighbor?

This Biblical question elicited the parable of the Good Samaritan, which presents the daunting ideal that we ought to behave as if all humans were our neighbors. That, in turn, implies that in Biblical times, presumably a time of community dominance, one would unhesitantly help a neighbor and expect such help in turn. On the other hand, the commandment "Love Thy Neighbor as Thyself" would imply that this degree of intimacy was not taken for granted.

It appears that this point of view was still held by scholars at the beginning of the twentieth century. Sociologists like Park, Burgess, and Wirth saw the neighborhood as a locus of intense loyalties and intimate involvements generating high levels of social cohesion. Neighbors knew one another, frequently interacted, and cared about each other (Fischer, 1984).

Both the Biblical discussion and the early sociologists, then, assumed proximity and focused on the social interactions as the determinants. When we get to later sociologists, oriented toward describing a social situation, we get a distinct change in tone. Ulf Hannertz (1980), for instance, notes that three essential elements to the neighbor relationship are proximity, awareness, and recognition. So the neighbor needs to have a spatial location, needs to live nearby. But that is not enough if we are not aware that another person is in the same neighborhood and acknowledge this in some way. If we meet the person who lives on our block downtown, do we nod or pass as strangers? The requirements seem to be less intense than those of earlier sociologists.

Hannertz suggests that neighborly relations may be described in terms of three kinds of rituals. There are rituals of deference and demeanor emphasizing norms of civility and consideration. Age and gender are likely to influence these interactions, perhaps social position if it is known by title or possibly conferred by language or self-projection. Neighborly relationships may also involve exchanges of goods or services: soup to the ill, tools to the maintainers, or services such as holding, steadying, or giving advice in home improvement, automotive mechanics, or cooking. Finally, and most subtly, neighboring involves controlling information between various "social" domains such as the household and the neighborhood or between individuals as a means of ordering relationships with respect to compatibility, the prestige order, and resources. Hannertz makes the interesting suggestion that the character of neighboring relationships is a product of a "chemistry of inside and outside roles of neighbors." It is the mix of these local and extralocal roles that determines the individual's involvement in and style of neighboring and the neighborhood's character.

Why do neighborhoods exist? If one has friends and family, what does it matter who lives next door or across the street, assuming that these physical neighbors do not interfere with the way in which one lives? Would it follow that those who are lacking friends and family would have more need for neighbors? Is neighborliness achieved at the cost of family ties? The same issue has been broached with respect to friendship (Fischer, 1984; Wellman, 1979). Or the question could be turned around. Could it be that in many cases the idea of a limited commitment to neighbors, as compared with family and friends, makes neighboring possible? One may greet people on the street and lend them a cup of flour without expecting to be drawn into their family feuds or psychological problems (Kasarda and Janowitz, 1974; Wellman and Leighton, 1979; Janowitz, 1952; Silverman 1987). And perhaps neighborhood is not crucial to well-being. What it provides may be found elsewhere (Wellman, 1979; Fischer, 1984).

It may be that neighboring relationships do not necessitate intimacy to the same extent as kinship and friendship; or it may be that neighborliness represents a different form of intimacy. It would be possible, then, for these three relationships to coincide, which would represent the essence of the urban village concept. Hunter (1975) makes a distinction between "just" neighbors and "real" neighbors in terms of cohesion, social integration, and the content of neighborly relationships. Much earlier McClenahan (1929) had distinguished between neighbors, those who interact with others in the same locale and those who do not—nighdwellers (Olson, 1982). Certainly some combination of friends, family, and neighbors provides social support that cannot be offered by trained professionals. Given the choice, people will turn to such groups for certain kinds of needs (Litwak and Szelenyi, 1969).

What kind of person is likely to be most neighborly, to be most supportive of others in the neighborhood, perhaps to expect or need more support? Fischer suggests that the typical neighborly person is more likely to be a long-time resident, in the process of raising a family, older, at home during the day, working class, living among others with similar values, statuses, etc. Silverman (1987), however, doubts the importance of family raising and day dwelling.

Long-time residency repeatedly turns up in research as a predictor of neighborhood attachment and involvement (Kasarda and Janowitz, 1974; Silverman, 1987). More study is needed on the contexts of that residence, particularly with reference to what might be called spatial affiliation: an extended temporal relationship with a place. Such affiliation involves a sense of rootedness and perhaps a feeling of ownership. It is generational and ideological. At the individual level it encompasses a sense of belonging and investment such as implied by the term *family farm*. It suggests an important contribution of place to personal identity, to one's understanding of who one is. In this sense it is familiar in nature. For some a place, whether house or neighborhood, may be something of an urban homestead. It may tie us to the past and to those now gone away. Hunter notes such symbolic attachment on the part of elderly residents in his Rochester study. A recent best seller by J. Anthony Lukas, *Common Ground* (1985), examines the effects of busing and other social changes upon various Boston families. Each of the protagonists had a remarkably long familial association with Boston, either directly or indirectly. And each had a strong feeling of belonging there. To what extent do such feelings affect neighboring?

While individuals may live near one another without being neighbors, or at any rate neighborly, it is not possible to be neighbors without sharing space. People share some agreement about the identity of a neighborhood based on recognized boundaries, history, similarities in land use and population, or administrative structures of authority. They may also share perceptions of threat from zoning changes or facility construction (Silverman, 1987). This does not necessarily mean they extend the label of neighbor to all residents or agree exactly on the boundaries. Perceptions of boundaries may even change over time as networks of friends and acquaintances change.

The nature of housing may have important effects on neighboring. Are the neighbors renters, with common perceptions of landlords as malevolent or benevolent forces? Do they share neighboring apartments with thin walls and common hallways? Or are they home owners with discrete property boundaries and a choice of how neighborly or private they wish to be, while also having a greater long-term commitment to the neighborhood (Zito, 1974; Olson, 1982; Silverman, 1987)?

Social scientists have attempted to deal with classification of space by proposing a "nested" neighborhood model (Slovak, 1986). Primary and secondary neighborhoods may be distinguished—for example, a block radius where children play within a wider area of homogeneous housing values. Both of these may be included in an area demarcated by neighborhood names, school districts, and transportation arteries, and these, in turn, are included in suburbs, townships, or submetropolitan regions (Birch, et. al. 1979; Galster, 1987).

The same symbolic meaning of place can be applied to a neighborhood, as Firey (1978) demonstrated many years ago. What is the "place" of neighborhood in the larger social order? Or more precisely, does it have a place? Is there a distinct local culture that locates the neighborhood in history as well as in the current order?

And if a person is permanently displaced, as so many Americans are, do the same longings still exist? Will some seek a neighborhood with a history and identify themselves with that history? While the long-time residents may remember how things were when they were children or what their parents told them of even earlier times, will the new middle class urban nomads, seeking roots, be the ones who replace their two-pane windows with six-over-six sash windows and frequent the local library to learn the history of the neighborhood, to acquire a history for themselves?

In much of the research on community change, the focus has been on the urban immigration of rural nomads, either village Europeans or Appalachians and African Americans from the rural South. But the growth of corporate society has created urban nomads too, company families who move frequently (Whyte, 1956). Some may be alienated by the visual formlessness of suburbia and seek, instead, a village near the city, if one can be found. Such a village, then, may experience reverse immigration, with the urbanite moving in on the villager.

The Boundaries of Neighborhood

Research tends to show that urbanites have more ties outside their community than do villagers (Kasarda and Janowitz, 1974; Tsai and Sigelman, 1982; Fischer, 1982; Silverman, 1987). Would this be the case when the villagers are the long-time residents, and the urbanites the immigrants?

As one crosses the boundaries of such imaginary concentric circles, one may feel less likely to greet individuals or meet a familiar face, but still feel at home because of familiar landmarks: the department store where one shops, the tallest or most beautiful church, the park shared by several neighborhoods. But neighboring is based on recognition of others in a shared space in a small-scale setting. There would seem to be real ecological limits on potential for neighboring. Kirkpatrick Sale (1980) believes that the human capacity for "knowing" others cannot exceed eight hundred to one thousand, with the norm in the range of three hundred to five hundred. Then, too, the human eye cannot recognize features of another person beyond 1500 feet, a factor that affects ordering relationships within a locality through the ability to distinguish strangers from neighbors.

Too often studies proceed from a definition of an area to questions about the area. For instance the question "Do any of your three best friends live in this (predefined) neighborhood?" may bring quite different results from the question "Where, on this map of the larger community, do your three best friends live?" The latter question, answered by a sufficient random sample, could produce a different neighborhood boundary. The same applies to kin, organizational participation, and other "neighboring" variables.

Does a neighborhood, then, occupy a "natural area" such as posited by Park and Burgess (1925)? Or is it better defined as a set of networks among people that, in turn, demarcates an area of shared interaction? (Olson, 1982) One determinant of neighborhood boundaries may be physical appearance. Boundaries of rivers, railroad tracks, or highways may be effectively visible boundaries. Or an area may be distinguished by a style of housing if it was built in a certain period after which styles changed. In such a case, would there be a common perception of the neighborhood, even if networks of friends cut across those boundaries? Once again, the possibility of neighbors having a different quality from friends and family must be considered. The appearance of community (social homogeneity) may provide an essential element in the feeling that one's home is a refuge from the stress of urban life and work (Wellman and Leighton, 1979).

It may be, too, that the neighborhood includes an institution, resource, or territory that is outside the neighborhood, or the nearest library if it happens to be outside the neighborhood. Or there may be a supermarket or mall, to which members of the neighborhood go, which hires their children and caters to the tastes of the residents. The nearest outpatient clinic or Social Security office may get all the neighborhood clients, or the nearest bank may draw all the neighbors on the same day. Thus neighbors could share usage and a sense of ownership in resources not in their own community. The consequences of "possession" of such extra local resources has been shown to enhance the prestige of a neighborhood, as was the case with the Italians studied by Suttles, or the Irish of Boston (Lukas, 1985).

It is also possible that an institution or resource used by outsiders is located within the neighborhood (Millfield's police station, for example). Such resources, to the extent that they are controlled by outsiders, may weaken local control and undermine local social organization. Most efforts of large, bureaucratic organizations, such as hospitals, universities, etc., to be "good neighbors" have not been successful except when personnel and/or clients have included part of the neighborhood population. It may be, too, that an external resource represents the loss of an internal resource. The sparkling new regional post office causes the closing of the old neighborhood post office. Or, perhaps the ultimate horror, the opening of a Kentucky Fried Chicken on the nearby highway causes the closing of Tally's Corner.

While the general literature has shown that the neighborhood has survived (Wellman and Leighton, 1979), there are many accounts of disintegrations of particular neighborhoods, sometimes literally from events such as urban renewal, sometimes relatively from the pull of outside areas of social attraction, or the disintegration of social control (Olson, 1982). Neighborhood changes can be dramatic, such as the exodus of the middle class from some city areas or the inundation of city or village areas by middle class urbanites, a process sometimes called gentrification. Such change can be viewed as progress from the viewpoint of the new arrivals, or as disintegration from the viewpoint of the older occupants (Feagin, 1973; Fischer, 1984; Powell, 1972; Tilly, 1978).

What About Millfield?

Before we consider what the residents of Millfield have to say, what does previous research lead us to expect? Millfield certainly looks like a community. You don't have to know the inner networks to see it. If one had a Wirthian sense of lost community, it certainly might seem to be a place of refuge. Is that what it is? But Millfield is not an urban village in the sense that Gans' North Boston was (1962). Though it is adjacent to bustling Coopertown and part of the greater Brixton area, it is visually autonomous, surrounded by cornfields that, as we shall see, are more beloved to its citizens than they are to the farmers who grow them. On the other hand, Millfield is no longer a village like Vidich and Bensman's Springdale (1958), though it once was. We have not cited rural studies as much as urban studies, because residents of Millfield are not farmers, though some may come from farming families. Whether the owners of the cornfields can be considered part of the village will depend on the friendship networks. Visually, the farmhouses are not clearly within the village.

We shall have to see if we can find out the relative power of friendship, kinship, and neighborliness in Millfield. And we shall have to see whether it is itself a single neighborhood or a community of neighborhoods. What do the residents think? And are their neighbors in fact their friends or family? Do they have closer relations with those who live on their street than those on the next block? Does it matter whether they have children or are home during the day? Are some people neighbors, others nighdwellers? Do local facilities, such as the post office, play an important role?

How self-contained is Millfield? Do the residents stay home on Saturday and improve their homes, or do they visit friends, shop in malls, or attend football games outside of the community? If they do, can we call Millfield a place of refuge? Does home ownership affect social relations? Is Millfield a community of limited liability despite its intimate appearance? Do the urbanites have more outside relationships that the established villagers? Is this compensated for by the villagers' longer residence and possibly greater network of kin in the surrounding area?

Has there been a decline in neighborhood solidarity? Will residents remember the good old days when people were closer together? Or have new people moved in with a stronger desire for neighboring than long-term residents? Will the newcomers seem like busybodies to the old-timers, who will look back to a day when people minded their own business? Will long-time residence work in reverse to the usual expectation of greater neighborliness? On the other hand, will status be correlated with neighboring? Will the urbanites moving in have a greater interest in preserving or improving the community?

Long-term residency research suggests that there may be several kinds of impulses. There may be long-term residents who have a sense of roots and belonging, who have stories to tell about the past. There may be long-term residents who are so comfortable in their environment that they live only in the present and are not concerned about the past. And there may be urban nomads seeking a past in Millfield that they could not find in Coopertown. Possibly, of course, there will be other urban nomads with no such sense of history, who bought a house in Millfield because it was cheap or near to their workplace.

Can we discern rituals of neighborliness such as Hannertz (1980) describes? Is there a conflict between maintaining the community and being free to pursue one's own life? Is there a tension between these objectives? Between people? Within the same individual? Are people united by shared problems, or do they have different interests? Are perceptions of Coopertown's zoning plans, for instance, threatening to some, reassuring to others?

Millfield has lost its family grocery store. Does the post office serve as an adequate substitute? Are the urbanites moving into Millfield and putting six over six sash windows in their houses similar to others who are buying and renovating houses in the downtown area? Is Millfield undergoing a process of gentrification? Do memories of the past affect residents' perceptions of Millfield? Does it make a difference whether they grew up in a village, a suburb, or the city?

Or is Millfield what it appears to be, a Park and Burgess neighborhood, a neighborhood such as Edward Shils (Olson, 1982: 510) described?

To live in a district in which one feels "at home," to have neighbors, even if they are not friends, who greet one and offer a friendly smile is good. It may not appear to be a massive fact of social structure but it does have something to do with the satisfaction which a human being gets out of life. It might not integrate directly into the national community and it might have nothing to do with "goals." But not everything that human beings do has "goals." The good may lie in the action itself, such as smiling, saying "Good Evening," chatting a few words about the weather or some other inconsequential subject.

Chapter III

The Perception of Community

Who Perceives Community?

We had wondered if Millfield appeals to us as urbanites. Is there something about the quaintness that calls to city dwellers but would be taken for granted by people who had always lived in villages or rural areas? If so, are urbanites moving in to experience this quaintness and will they undercut their objective by urbanizing the village? In the process, does the city house buyer drive up prices, and in improving their houses drive up taxes, and ultimately drive out the villager who had lived there? If that happens, are the long-time residents fearful or resentful of the immigrant?

Or is this an exaggerated picture of conflict derived from the gentrification experience of the city? If prices go up somewhat, the village dweller may be content to sell because Millfield would not be that special to him. And even if the price of housing were to rise, taxes may not change dramatically, because the need for home improvement is far less that it would be in a gentrifying city neighborhood. Whereas the gentrifier sees possibilities in a Victorian shell, the immigrant to Millfield would be purchasing a thirty- to eighty-year-old house ready to live in and would not have to invest the cost of a house in making repairs. Moreover, those who live there may remain. If they do move, it may be because the offering prices for houses are high.

We might suspect, then, that immigrants to Millfield would be content to be villagers without seeking gentry status. They would be attracted by the sense of community, the beauty, the coziness that provides an enclave of peace at the edge of the lively but enervating urban area. Perhaps they buy their homes from rural residents who see Millfield somewhat differently, as the place where

Table III-1

Reasons for Moving to or Remaining in Millfield

Reasons	Number	Percentage
Community	12	50%
House	12	50%
Family	12	50%
Location	4	17%

childhoods were spent, where their families live, perhaps as a place a little outmoded in comparison with the brick ranches with big lawns that characterize the rest of Coopertown and other greater Brixton suburbs. Do the urban immigrants perhaps find solace in walking to the post office to pick up their mail and greeting a rural neighbor, a neighbor who perhaps feels mail ought to be delivered to a mailbox, as it is in the rest of Coopertown? Do the immigrants take a dim view of the junked automobile that undermines the beauty of the community, a car perhaps owned by a native neighbor who staunchly believes that each person has the right to do as he or she wishes with private property?

Our hypothesis, then, is that there would be a different sense of community between the native villager, who has lived and grown up in Millfield or its rural environs, and the urban immigrant, who moves in from greater Brixton or some other part of the country and chooses Millfield as a place to live precisely because it appears to be a community oasis in a desert of ranches.

Why Choose Millfield?

We guessed that Millfield was being invaded by urban immigrants who wanted to live in a village. We anticipated, therefore, that community would be their first reason for moving there. A second reason might be that housing would be cheaper compared to the rest of the greater Brixton area. We did not anticipate that there would be many people left who were born there and we did not expect that the location of Millfield would be important, except as compared with country towns farther from the metropolis.

So we asked why people had moved to Millfield or, if they had always lived there, why they had stayed. This question came early in the questionnaire, before we had given any indication of what our areas of concern might be. Table

III-1 shows their generalized response. It turned out that community, family, and housing were of equal concern. Each was mentioned in exactly half the households. Location, as expected, was of less importance.

Those who referred to community particularly noted the size and atmosphere of the village, characteristics that were immediately apparent on a first visit. Typical comments included "...such a little town," "...small, little village...," "...shrubbery and trees all around...," "And we just liked the town. And it was, well, you seen what it is. It's just nice lookin'."

They also referred frequently to knowing and liking the neighbors, though that was less specifically spelled out, and in one case a contrary message was delivered. For the woman who thought the town was nice looking went on to add that "the people are friendly. Everybody 'bout knows everybody." But the man who praised the shrubbery and the trees added "...so you sit in your yard and not even see your neighbors." Another resident seemed to agree with both points of view. "It's quiet and everybody's friendly, minds their own business."

A few referred to safety, trust, and absence of problems caused by strangers. "...You can leave stuff sit out, like, on the porches, and nobody bothers us." A man who had lived in Brixton and parked his car on the street remarked that it then had "a lot of dents in it."

Of those concerned with the house itself, size and price were most frequently mentioned. "It was something we could afford." Others liked the size for what it cost; they needed something bigger for a growing family; or the newly married needed something small for two people. Or they rented from parents and got a good deal.

Antiquity was also mentioned. They were looking for an old-type farmhouse. They wanted a house that would go with antiques. Or they wanted an old house they could remodel. But, as anticipated, remodeling houses was not a major factor. Besides the woman who wanted to remodel the old house, there was one man who bought what he "could afford, an old house in terrible condition."

Of course, even in a sample of twenty-four, there are going to be cases that defy classification. One husband said his wife wanted to get out of Corinth after a tornado had struck the city. "That's the reason!" his wife exclaimed. "This place was for sale," he said, "and it had a basement, so...we bought it." Another couple bought because of a corner cabinet. They peeped in the window of a house "and she saw the corner cabinet setting there so that's what sold us on this house."

It is difficult to render what was not said. The question gave no lead, there was no multiple choice, so a person did not have to deliberately exclude community. But given the striking aspect of Millfield as compared with its environment, was it possible to consider a house without any reference to its

TABLE III-2

Did Not Mention Community

Reason	Number	out of	Total Percentage
House but not community	6	12	50%
Family but not community	5	12	42%
Family and house but not community	3	4	75%

setting? Was it possible to speak of growing up in the area (usually referring to Coopertown) or of one's family living in Millfield without any reference to the community? As Table III-2 indicates, indeed it was. Half of those who mentioned house and almost half who referred to family did not mention the community.

We expected an association of house and community. A couple came out to Millfield because they had heard about "some old-type farmhouses that would be available." They found such a house, but "we also liked the atmosphere, small little village..." But many times we had responses like this. A couple bought the house after her husband was transferred to a military base outside of Brixton. "Still," the questioner pursued, "Millfield is a bit away from the base, isn't it?" "The reason was," the wife replied, "we found this old house and it was something we could afford." Now this house stands halfway down Millfield Road, right in the middle of the village in a very attractive setting. But the setting was not mentioned.

Another who knew some of the neighbors from having gone to school in Coopertown days said he bought his house because he needed more room for his children. The questioner summed up by saying that neither community nor location were factors and the respondent agreed.

So in the open-ended question, where any factor or factors could have been chosen, community was no more important than house or family. And not all who referred to community were enthusiastic. As one questioner summed it up: "You like the area, like the neighborhood, not your ideal, but for the money it came closest."

Millfielder: "Right."

Who Sees Community?

The initial image we had was of a village invaded by urban immigrants, better-educated people with higher-paying jobs replacing area villagers. If that was the case, these urbanites seeking community had not yet overwhelmed the village. And we did indeed find a few who had always lived in Millfield, and others who went to school in Coopertown and eventually settled in Millfield. The next question to be answered was: Were those who perceived community generally the urban immigrants? Perhaps the process is going on, but at an earlier phase. The immigrants have not yet overwhelmed the natives.

If that is the case, Millfield may be undergoing a quiet social revolution of the kind that has seen the urban villager replaced by the urban gentry. The urban conflicts, however, have been highly visible and often emotional: the gentry are often rich and white, the villagers poor and from ethnic or racial minorities.

In Millfield, there is hardly a visible conflict. The gentry and the villagers are white (there is one black family in Millfield) and the disparity in income is probably not great, or at any rate strikingly visible. There are differences, however, that the questionnaire should reveal. Some speak the urban grammar of the English textbook; some are more colloquial. We wondered if there would be a correlation between those who mentioned community and those who have more education, higher working status, and spoke textbook English. And to what extent were they the ones who moved in from some other area? Had they moved in more recently, in the 1970s or 1980s? Were they likely to be younger?

As Table III-3 shows, the results were not very impressive. In the total sample, twelve of the twenty-four families had mentioned community as a reason for moving to Millfield or staying. The expectation that those who were immediately conscious of community would be young, college-educated, upper-middle class, textbook-speaking outsiders didn't receive much support.

Only two of these categories was mildly supported. Sixty percent of those who had upper-middle class occupations and more than 60 percent of those under fifty mentioned community. Would that percentage be improved by moving the age back to forty? No, it dropped under 60 percent when that was done. None of the other categories was over 60 percent and one—the outsiders—fell under 40 percent. The outsiders were defined as those households in which neither partner came from Millfield or Coopertown. When we turned it around and considered those households in which at least one partner was from Coopertown, only 55 percent mentioned community, so the inverse of the hypothesis was not supported either.

It would appear, then, that the image of a wealthier, younger, more urbanized class taking over the village of Millfield is not supported by the interviews. Some urbanites moved in for that reason, but some of the old-time villagers also moved in or remain because they like the community. The young

TABLE III-3

Who Mentioned Community

Factor	Mentioned Community	No Mention of Community	Percentage
Total sample	12	12	50%
Moved within 15 years	6	6	50%
From Brixton or outside	5	8	38%
One from Millfield or Coopertown	6	5	55%
Three years of college or more	4	5	44%
Textbook language	6	5	55%
Upper-middle class occupation	6	4	60%
Age under 50	9	5	64%
Both under 40	4	3	57%

are more likely to perceive community than the elderly, but the young have to be defined as those under fifty. Some with middle class occupations, college educations, and textbook language quickly perceive community, but just about as many do not.

One other possibility occurred to us in considering the circumstances in which people might move into Millfield. Was it possible that the idea of community would appeal more to women than to men? The image would be of the wife looking at the beauty and homeliness of the community while her husband was considering number of rooms, dryness of cellar, mortgage advantages, and space for storing and using tools. Did it turn out that the females were more likely to mention community? No, in the twelve households that community was mentioned, it was in each case mentioned by only one member. Five of these were women; seven were men.

Conclusion

On the basis of this initial investigation, there would seem to be varying motivations for living in Millfield, and no clear-cut cleavages. Some people say they live there for community; some do not. But about half of those who mentioned family background also mentioned community, and half of those who came looking for a particular house were also aware of community. Living in Millfield a long time or searching for a particular kind of house did not necessarily blind the residents to the charms of the community.

Apparently, too, there is no pattern of previous residence, education, language, occupation, age, or gender in relation to initial perceptions of Millfield's community. Community was as evident to the long-time resident as to the immigrant, to the high school-educated as to the college graduate, to the colloquial speaker as to the textbook speaker, to the labor and service occupied as to the manager or professional, to the older person as to the younger, to men as to women. It was evident, but not overwhelming, not the first factor in everyone's mind.

On first inspection, then, it would appear that what you see is what you get. Millfield's community is appreciated by many of the residents, but it is not the most important consideration for everyone. The community is pleasant, but apparently not overwhelming; nor is there evidence of an overwhelming or even incipient community takeover by urban invaders.

CHAPTER IV

Community Image Versus Urban Activity

According to the literature on community, we would expect that neighbors will be supportive of one another, mutually committed to the community, but more intensely concerned about family and friends. Even though community came to mind in only half the households interviewed, we would expect that when the subject of community is specifically addressed that people in Millfield would respond to it positively. It would be surprising if there were a strong negative response.

But we would expect that on Saturday, when the opportunity for community interaction was present, Millfielders would spend more time with family and friends than with other Millfielders. Nor would we be surprised if they interacted less with one another than they realized. This comes closer to the launching pad idea, though that military analogy is incomplete. Not only would we expect Millfielders to be launched into activities outside the community, but we should also expect others from outside to be launched into Millfield. A better analogy might be a trading map, where a given city sends forth beer, fur, and timber and gets back textiles, spices, and beeswax.

Our expectation, then, was that most people would have kin in the greater Brixton area and many would be encountered. We also expected that the interaction of the nuclear family would be more intense than neighborly relations. We expected, however, that this tendency might be more pronounced among long-time residents than among those who had moved in during the past decade. We did not expect that Millfield would be either village or urban community. At first glance it may look like Vidich and Bensman's Springdale, except that families living in Millfield get their economic support from somewhere else and don't need the village as a center of their social life.

In other respects it may resemble a gentrifying area of the inner city. But the people moving in are not racially or economically distinguishable from those who live there, and perhaps on weekends they even adopt the villagers' dress, overalls rather than jeans. Nor would the owner-renter distinction be as strongly drawn as it would be in a gentrifying community, nor are the houses in obvious need of repair. In appearance they are already acceptably middle class.

It seemed likely, therefore, that most people living in Millfield would perceive it to be a friendly, neighborly place, with a great deal of social interaction going on. They would also see it as a haven of peace and seclusion from city bustle. But in fact their busy lives, both on weekdays and weekends, would keep them from either socializing or experiencing much of the tranquility the village seemed to offer.

We asked about the perceptions of Millfield—why they lived there, how they felt about their neighbors, the circumstances under which they met with other residents of Millfield, changes they experienced and expected. We expected they would convey that Millfield was a warm, friendly, supportive, and beautiful place in which everybody knew everybody else. Then we asked about activities. What did you do yesterday (a Friday) and today (a Saturday)? We expected that actual activities would more frequently take place outside Millfield rather than within the village.

Atmosphere

It turned out that residents of almost all the households perceived something special about Millfield. They particularly remarked on what we might call the atmosphere and their relationships with their neighbors. The atmosphere included the size of the village, a feeling of peace compared with the rest of greater Brixton, pleasure in the appearance, perceptions of internal coherence, and a feeling of safety within the village. In twenty of the households, remarks fitting in one or more of these categories were made.

The size was referred to favorably by several. "Such a nice little town," "a small little village," a "nice little community," "more of a little country town than it is a city." The size of the community is associated with other factors: Because it is small, you know your neighbors at least by sight, and therefore can recognize strangers, which in turn contributes to safety. The residents perceive that there is very little crime. "You can leave stuff sit out, like, on the porches, and nobody bothers it." There are no kids "destroying things," no neighborhood watch needed. The children are safe too. On Halloween "a person would feel safe...having their kids in an area like this. They wouldn't have to take a magnet and go through the candy..." "Kids can play outside all day long. Nobody bothers them." And women are safe too. "I feel very safe when my husband and boys are gone late at night, with the neighbors right here,

I feel it's a very safe place."

Some consider homogeneity desirable. "I've enjoyed the neighborhood. It's very close knit. Even those who appear to be different really aren't." Newcomers are seen as fitting in. They "like the atmosphere, the homes they purchase and want to maintain, those people are the majority. They blend in with the old-timers here..." In other words, all are committed to maintaining the village as it is, keeping up their homes, friendliness, trust, safety. Even Millfield's single African American household elicits bemusement rather than alarm. "Well, it was all white until about ten years ago...We don't know how he got here," remarked one respondent. Quickly adding, "He's real nice, you know..." But there is also a hint of concern about newcomers, a vague feeling of suspicion about the Historical Society: "The newer people that's got in...they're trying to change it to a, (to his wife) what is it?" "Historical." "Historical thing now." But the Historical Society is committed to preservation: Why should that be a worry?

Another older resident put it like this. "I don't think Millfield will ever change unless the city comes in and starts saying 'You're going to have to do this, you're going to have to do that,' because being an old village like it is, see that fellow over there, he's got old cars and I have chickens and ducks." These comments were about as close as anyone came to criticizing the Historical Society, which certainly was started by relative newcomers, but also has its proponents among older residents. Brixton newspapers, over the past decade, have included articles about controversies over rules proposed by historical societies concerning types of fences, doors, or roofs that would be permitted in a community.

Knowing the residents means knowing the strangers. One resident blocks his street with his truck so strangers can't drive down it. "You see, a car, a stranger just went through there, you see, well see, now he's out of his car. I figure a guy's looking like that, especially if they're in old cars like that (Millfield abounds in old cars), they're looking for something to steal. But I'm not blocking anybody else...cuz the other people can get out the other end of the street." And his wife added: "Anybody moves into the neighborhood and starts 'hot-rodding' up and down that street, why some of us would get together and try to put a stop to it very quickly." These mild anxieties about newcomers and strangers are hardly pervasive. These slightly worried comments came from only two households.

Part of the perception of the community, for the residents as for the outsider, is in the appearance of the village. On the one hand there seems to be a great deal of unanimity about this. People want the community to remain as it is. They generally agree that it is attractive. "Well, you seen what it is," said one long-time resident, "it's just nice lookin'." Many others spoke of the atmosphere.

But there was also a frequently conveyed perception that compared with the past, the village is a bit run down. One long-time resident spoke of Hickory Street with regret. "It was beautiful down there when I lived down there," (in the 1930s) she said. "It's run down since we lived there." Even her own postcard house doesn't seem to her to be what it once was. From the lot across the street, "they painted this place. And it was beautiful, the paintings they had of it." Does it live only in paintings? Do they not paint it anymore?

Another long-time resident said there were a few houses at the other end of the village in need of repair. He could also have been referring to the same side street. If so, the residents of Hickory Street did not view decline but rather noted improvements. One noted with satisfaction, "The lady next door put the sidewalks in which the town should've done...my neighbors are really building this street up." A female respondent born in Millfield and living on Hickory Street would like to have city services, like street lights, since she is paying city taxes. But sidewalks and street lights may not be what the members of the Millfield Society have in mind. Keeping the village as it was would not include those conveniences, nor mailboxes. Historical Society members stress, rather, fixing up houses, repairing porches, and restoration. They think this is happening more and more as new people move in. Older residents approve of that, so long as it doesn't get too fancy, and so long as codes are not imposed that prevent people from doing what comes naturally. "I think the Millfield Society...is going to try to continue...keeping Millfield similar to what it is. Natural homes, not modern homes going in or anything like that." But still home, as one remarked, should be "a place that you can come in, you can sit down, you're not afraid to step on the carpet or anything else." In his backyard, he "tinkles with cars and it's a cyclone, looks like it is now."

Yet, regardless of how his yard may look, he nevertheless fears a development being put in the cornfield across the street and thinks a lot of people in Millfield feel that way. "That's the reason we moved out here, so we could see a cornstalk across...If we wanted to live in an upper-level development area, then we'd a moved there."

So there seems to be agreement that the village should not include or be adjacent to modern houses. There is some difference about whether there should be modern city conveniences added. And some fear that the desire for restoration could lead to enforcement of the who-knows-what zoning ordinances that may be on the books in Coopertown. The man who likes both tinkering and cornfields summed it up: "I just think that now it would look a little far fetche to put split-levels or ranch-style houses over there and these older houses ov here. And I'm not a big proponent of this historical village thing. I mean, I guess I'm kinda greedy. I like the best of two worlds."

Both long-time residents and newcomers referred to peace, to tranquility, and to the possibility of getting away from the rest of the world. Mom and Dad from the city "like to come out and just sit on the swing and watch the cars go by and stuff, ya know. Because it's more leisurely...they just come out and enjoy themselves...It gives you a little retreat to get away from the hustle and bustle of every place else." Another resident asserted, "...You can sit outside on the weekends and all you hear is the sounds of nature out there. Once in a while you'll hear a car go by." One native-born Millfielder said, "Maybe it's a feeling of peace that I get from the trees. Ever since I was a little girl, I've always loved the trees." Her sentiments are echoed by a recent immigrant: "I love it! It's great. It's neat. Laid back...The solitude. The quiet, tranquility. I can't believe it, you can't believe what it's like to be sitting here in the quiet."

We mentioned that in only four households was there no reference to community. How can there be no perception of community in a place like Millfield? It isn't easy to illustrate an absence of something, but consider this comment on change: "Well, of course you don't have trains like we used to. This street used to be a gravel road. This was only a four-room house but now it is a six-room house. Well, just a host of things. People change every year. They come and go."

"Would you say you have been satisfied with Millfield?"

"Very much. The only bad part around here is the mosquitoes."

Neighbors

"And the people are friendly. Everybody 'bout knows everybody."

"You can sit in your yard and not even see your neighbors..."

These two comments sum up the parameters of perceptions of neighbors. Everybody knows everybody is a perception of a long-time resident who pretty nearly does know everybody, at least to the extent that she would notice a stranger. Sitting in your yard and not seeing your neighbors represents a competition between the demands of community and other demands of life, including those of privacy and peace. In this competition, one gets the impression that community is not overwhelmingly intrusive; it can be set aside when other demands seem more important.

All but two of the households responded favorably when asked about neighbors. Only one person responded negatively. But there were recurrent reservations about frequency and depth. One couple said, "We really like the people here" when asked why they stayed in Millfield. But later, when asked about their neighbors, they said they had limited contact, only socialized with one. They talked with others who they saw around or stopped by. They had the feeling that they saw fewer people because of their location at one end of the village or because others had lived there longer. But cumulatively their experience was typical. Neighbors dropped by, met at the post office, waved as they went by, but didn't come over for dinner or cards.

"I can't picture living away from Millfield...because everyone knows everyone else and...they wave to you when they go by."

"People walk around and say hi and maybe come up on your porch and talk for ten minutes." "And everybody's busy too." "Well, everybody's workin' on their house."

"I wouldn't say we talk to (the neighbors) an awful lot. If they happen to come by going to the post office and we're out there in front, they stop...just visit for a little while."

One woman who worked didn't see much of her neighbors, but thought she was atypical. "I would think that they'd probably be a lot more open and friendly...it's just that I'm never here."

Children get into one another's houses, but rarely adults. "We don't play cards with anybody or anything like that." One who said he didn't visit neighbors' homes nevertheless said that, even in the winter, "you see somebody and you just kinda wave and say 'hi, how've you been? What's new?'...I mean you're just not really neighbor neighbors. Do you know what I mean?" There is a somewhat apologetic tone here, as if in Millfield more should be expected than a wave. But others, perhaps with different previous experience, seem to think this is an outstanding characteristic of Millfielders.

"And they meet ya," one woman said, "and ya laugh and talk...and they invite ya over to speak to ya...even if they're going someplace, they'll talk to ya a few minutes before they leave. Holler at ya, and if you're on the porch they're always wavin' or blowin' a horn at ya or something." Or the oil men "wave, and it's not a business wave, ya know, it's a friendly wave...And I think that's the atmosphere...that's probably the drawing thing that brought people to Millfield."

More than half of the residents referred to helping one another out, sometimes immediately after commenting that they didn't have much to do with neighbors. "I don't know why I should talk about (the neighbors). I don't know them. Don't mess with them." But, of course, if "there's been a death around here in the neighborhood, families go together. The church, they take food and stuff in like that. If they're sick they try to help 'em out."

"If you are sick, somebody usually shows up."

When the man across the street "passed away, I got on the phone and called all of the neighbors" and "they brought food in."

"If someone is sick, people will show up with chicken soup." Made from a fresh-killed Millfield chicken, one feels.

The most common type of help is looking after a neighbor's property. If "a stranger comes to your neighbor's house and you know he's not home you're gonna look and see what's going on." Other Millfielders noted, "There's a lot of taking care of each other's houses when people go away, feeding the cats and dogs and just keeping an eye out" and "we watch and make sure don't nobody steal nothing."

Children are watched as well as cats. Sometimes younger couples care for one anothers children, but one grandmotherly type said she "keeps other peoples' kids and don't charge just for the enjoyment of keepin' the kids around and the kids come over to visit us sometimes too.... We have some chickens and kids like them baby chickens."

Borrowing and helping with work also goes on, though some of the older residents feel this has declined. One man commented that if he needs to borrow a tool from the local garage "I can walk down...and get it and come back and use the thing." A woman said, "Bill and I do a lot of help and trading and work...I would say maybe several of us do it more than the majority." Another who thinks there is less working together says that he and his neighbor "work back and forth together. If he needs me, I'll let my stuff go and go down and help him. It works the same way with him for me." Further comments include, "If the neighbors come and say they need something, they just go in the garage and get it" and "You know, people before, they used to help each other, but the people today, you just can't find people that's willing to help. I'm one that I'd help anybody." One woman agreed that help was declining. She thought a lot of older women now work and "that makes it hard for them."

The one man who did not think there was much neighborly interaction added, "I don't get much help...I think it's the attitude towards me." But while some may have thought they helped more than they were helped, there seemed to be a widespread perception that help was there for the asking. "I mean everybody here is very neighborly," one man said, "and all you have to do if you want somebody to help you out is ask, you know, they'll be more than glad to do it." "I think the majority are like that," added his wife. Another man had this image: "If somebody was to get on a...wagon and say, all right everybody in Millfield, ya know, we're gonna have to push a lead ball from here to Brixton, that everybody'd take their turn at pushin' it."

Where?

Under what circumstances do Millfielders encounter one another? Two circumstances seemed more common than others: going to the post office and visiting with neighbors. Two-thirds of the households mentioned the post office.

"The post office is the center. It's nice having it."

An older woman, living near the post office, commented, "I stand at the window and watch people go in....In the summertime if I'm out in the yard...they'll come over and talk to me before they go in the post office....If it wasn't there, if they closed that up, I'd really miss it."

"Of course I always see people when I go to the post office and I talk to Alice (the postmistress) and she always tells me about things."

One of the two residents in town who gets mail delivered had the impression that the post office was a particular center for women. Looking back at the comments, his impression was mildly confirmed by something like a 3:2 ratio.

Not everyone is enamored with the post office. One man, at least, dissented. "A lot of people, even the new residents in Millfield, like the quaintness and the thing of sayin' hey, I can go to the post office and get my mail, ya know. I guess they got in the back of their mind that, a New England farm town or somethin' and they're gonna take the sled down there and get the mail." The trouble is if you are away for a few days, your "pigeon hole looks like a disaster area...I just as soon they deliver the mail to the front porch".

More than half the households mentioned interaction with neighbors. Such interaction, however, did not necessarily involve the community as a whole. It could have taken place in any city or suburb where neighborhoods exist. People chatted on weekends when they worked in their yards, or they crossed the street and sat a while on someone else's front porch.

"You're always talking to neighbors right around."

"Whenever anyone is working in the yard."

"Just any time you see a neighbor out, you stand around and talk to 'em a while."

"Be out in the yard and they'll...walk across."

"We share a driveway and I go over and talk to them you know."

"Two people right across the street...they both have little children so we kind of have a nice little kids' gathering." The husbands work on cars together. "They also play the guitar and my husband is also involved musically so they talk a lot about that. I have a common bond with the mothers because of the children." Three young couples were bound by children and a couple of common interests. But this was the only case that surfaced in these interviews.

There were, however, equally strong neighborly bonds between a bachelor and a family with two sons. According to the husband, his wife and the bachelor "have a standing feud over this walnut tree out here, 'cause she doesn't like it hittin' her car...so every mornin' when she gets up there's two or three walnuts sittin' on top of her car. Now they've been placed there neatly; they haven't fallen." And his younger son regards his neighbor as "next to God, ya know; because he can work on cars and...he paints motorcycles...so my youngest one thinks that the sun rises and falls on him."

There were a number of references to Millfielders walking by and waving or stopping to chat, but it was hard to say whether they were also going to or from the post office, or whether they were or were not neighbors.

Two residents referred to disasters like a fire or a train derailment that got everyone out to see what happened. "Those kind of things bring us together." Only one referred to community activities, and that was to say she had been invited but had not been able to go.

One man mentioned that men used to meet at a restaurant immediately outside Millfield in Coopertown, but the restaurant had since closed. He also mentioned the local garage as a meeting place for young men.

Community Activities

Though community activities were rarely mentioned when people were asked about where people got together, or when asked about specific community activities, they tended to respond positively. In fourteen of the households there were favorable remarks about such activities. Only two said there were no such activities. One, a teenager, meant that there were none that interested her. Six others indicated that they did not go to community activities because of other interests, because of cost, or because they didn't care about them.

In nine of eleven houses on Millfield Road, the village main street, attitudes were positive. In only four of twelve households not on the main street were they unambiguously positive.

It was October when the interviews were conducted, and the most positive response was directed toward the community Halloween party. "Rather than lettin' 'em just run around there wherever, they have a Halloween. We have cider and stuff like that...and the kids all there playin' games and all. And everybody enjoying themself...Ya really have a nice time." In Corinth you might have two hundred kids at Halloween, "where here the kids that we have show up are the kids whose parents we all know." "On Beggars night...they pick one of the houses and they serve hot chocolate and cookies for the kids...and the parents are allowed to go (and have some) and that brings a lot of people together."

Other activities mentioned were summed up by one of the residents. "We got together and...had a picnic, we had one this year, we had one last year. We had a yard sale, everybody, we had a clean up Millfield and area, everyone worked on it. It was very enjoyable."

The man who puts walnuts on his neighbor's car mentioned the picnic and "trash dump." "I make a good hermit," he said, "but I do enjoy social encounters." Another who hadn't participated planned to do so to get "a little bit more in tune with the neighborhood...I'm kinda looking forward to it." Another man felt that the activities made socializing more natural. "I don't believe that it would seem right to say, okay now, every Tuesday night we're all gonna meet, ya know...and just sit down and chit-chat and stuff."

Those who did not participate certainly were not overtly critical. One couldn't afford the donation. "When you got a limited income you gotta watch what you're doing." Others indicated that time was scarce. "I got so many other interests." "We are interested for a short time. I don't like to spend hours there." "They always hold 'em about the time we're doing somethin' else." There was one resident who felt he should participate more. "I should because I am one of the older residents but I never got into things like that." Others didn't. "I just don't worry about 'em." "We don't care." Asked about activities, one household reflected the veiled reservation occasionally encountered about the Historical Society. "Just that little club they have. And not everybody is in it, so. They don't do a whole lot."

The response to activities seems to be favorable on the whole, but as compared with day-to-day encounters, not central to the coherence of the community. Overall, one has the impression of low-level, unpressured community interaction. People like the atmosphere of the village; they encounter their neighbors casually but don't feel pressured by intrusion. They see them across the way or on the way to the post office; they encounter them when they participate in community activities, which are pleasant, but infrequent, and not at all compulsory. Millfield is perceived as an oasis of friendliness in a busy and impersonal world, a place where you can relax and be friendly, or go about your own affairs, as you choose.

But What Did You Really Do?

After asking about various perceptions of Millfield, we asked the residents what they actually had done the previous day and what they had done or expected to do on the day of the interview. Since all interviews were conducted on Saturday, we had a sample weekday followed by a sample weekend day. Our expectation was that despite the perception residents had that they lived in a friendly community, they actually spent relatively little time socializing in the community and most of their time outside it, either working, shopping, or having fun. After all, charming though it may be, Millfield contains only two small businesses. So when residents worked or carried on other activities, they would have to go outside the village. And we expected the demands on time of work, of kin, of house maintenance and rehabilitation would, for busy Americans, wipe out most of the time that Millfielders would like to use for socializing. The image might be of sitting on the front porch watching the world go by, but the fact would be that the Millfielder was part of the world that was going by, not the country gentry they might like to be.

In exploring this hypothesis, you would not expect quantitative measure to be of much use. When you describe what you did yesterday, you describe what is salient. You may not notice many of the things that are second nature. So we simply wrote down the descriptions as they were given, noting which occurred in Millfield and which occurred outside. Then, of those that occurred within, how much really involved community or neighborly exchange? And if it did not occur on a random Friday or Saturday, when would it occur? We began by dividing the responses into four types: yesterday away and today away, then yesterday at home and today at home.

Sixteen Millfielders reported working the previous day in various places outside of Millfield and two teenagers went to Coopertown High School. Two worked into the night and one worked a night shift. They said very little about their work. Only one responded by giving any indication of what had happened in the course of the work day. This could have been a function of the contexts of the interview since people were being interviewed at home and were thinking about Millfield as a result of other questions. Also, in other research we have done with people at work, we have found them very interested in that work. All the same, while there was consistently no comment on the activities of work, there was comment on the details of other kinds of activities that took place outside of Millfield.

Seven Millfielders mentioned going for goods or services. The services for three women consisted of having their hair done. Four mentioned shopping for groceries. One couple bought the wife a coat at a garage sale and another couple bought the husband a pair of shoes. Three couples went to restaurants outside of Millfield on Friday night. A woman and her mother went to a luncheon in greater Brixton. One of the sons went with a friend to McDuff's House of Beer in Coopertown and a daughter went with friends to a Coopertown restaurant for pizza after the high school football game. The football game was the only mention of spectator entertainment. Two teenage girls went to that. But one older couple did go fishing during the day.

Seven households mentioned socializing and visiting, mostly with relatives. One woman visited her sister-in-law in Corinth. A man helped his brother-in-law paint a cabin in a village outside the Brixton area. A woman cleaned her mother-in-law's house. A daughter visited her grandmother in the greater Brixton area. A couple played cards at the wife's cousin's in Corinth. A grandmother and her sister and brother-in-law returned by plane from Las Vegas, where they had visited her children and grandchildren, who had flown in from Phoenix. Only one couple, spending the evening at the VFW in Coopertown, socialized outside Millfield without mentioning kin.

On Saturday there was more shopping with nine households involved. This included grocery shopping, dry cleaning, stopping at the bank, and paying bills. Male and female involvement was about equal, compared with Friday when most of the shoppers were women. One adult and one child visited doctors. Children were taken to skating lessons and football practice.

Several were involved in work, some of which implied socializing. A mechanic was going to work on a customer's car, but she promised him a dinner. One man helped others put up a flagpole at the VFW, and his wife was going to help prepare food at the VFW for more than two hundred people. A couple made a trip to a town outside the Brixton area to put in a window light in the house of the wife's friend. A young mechanic had already taken a motor to a shop in Brixton, and another young man who had returned from a class at the Brixton Community College now planned to help his (probably Coopertown) brother-in-law move furniture. A county public works superintendent was on maintenance call from a Coopertown nursing home. A daughter was going to work at a Catholic retreat in Coopertown, where her brother was already working. A wife had gone to manage a Coopertown fabrics store.

Others looked forward to various kinds of entertainment. A couple with a baby was going to a college town outside the Brixton area to enjoy its streets and parks. Two men had already been to a Coopertown restaurant "and found out all the gossip." A young man was getting ready to drag race at a track in Coopertown and his father would go along to watch the races. A man was going to watch his grandson play football in the Corinth Peewee League, and then go shopping. A son planned to go to McDuff's, but he was not the same one who had gone the night before. A woman planned to go with her husband to a retirement dinner outside the area. No one had played or planned to play golf. In only one household were all activities carried out in Millfield: that was the household of the seventy-five-year-old widow.

Activities in Millfield

There were, however, still a substantial number of activities carried out within the confines of Millfield. With varying numbers in households reporting, there doesn't seem to be any meaningful quantitative measurement possible, but in terms of notes taken, activities within and activities outside occupied about the same amount of space, with perhaps an edge to activities within. And if only one household reported no activities outside of Millfield, there was only one household that did not spend some time in Millfield beyond sleeping and eating meals. The walnut bachelor was apparently only at home to sleep, shower, and talk to a visiting sociologist.

Eleven households on Friday and fifteen on Saturday reported some kind of work going on around the house. Despite an image some Millfielders have of people restoring their houses, only one on each day reported any such activity. One couple, who referred to such activity on the part of others, were going to "clean out the bookshelves and strip the floors and sand them and refinish them...by the end of the day we'll be so tired." Another man worked on his house inside and outside in unspecified ways on Friday. Two others reported doing touch-up work, painting, and trimming, but nothing approaching restoration. Much more common were maintenance chores: yard work, feeding chickens, house cleaning, cooking, laundry, rehanging pictures, sawing wood, hair washing, and "odds and ends around the house."

There was not much creative work of the kind one didn't have to do. One woman crocheted, another was heavily into sewing clothes for herself, a third vegetable gardened. Aside from necessary cooking, there was a woman who was going to make noodles and a man expecting to clean the fish he and his wife had caught. A few residents did do some work relating to outside activities. The young man who was going to drag race worked on his car and also did some auto repair work that may have been for customers in or out of Millfield. A man chopped wood for his daughter who lived in Coopertown. A couple were getting things ready for a community garage sale coming up. The woman returning from Las Vegas unpacked. A woman was preparing for a church picnic Sunday. A young man studied for his college classes and two women prepared for Sunday School.

Thirteen households reported spending some leisure time at home on Friday, eleven on Saturday. Some didn't do anything or weren't going to: "just pooped out." Nine mentioned watching or planning to watch TV, with baseball playoffs and cartoons mentioned more frequently than anything else. Four mentioned reading. Doing nothing may have been related to the cherished "Millfield peace" mentioned by several. "This is a nice community to get away to instead of having a cabin somewhere at the lake or something, you can come right home and relax." (The couple who said this were doing this in the late afternoon when the interviewer came along.) Several mentioned taking it easy or sleeping late. Two were recovering from illnesses.

Children were somewhat involved in activities. Residents took babies for strolls and took older children places, as mentioned above. One woman mentioned getting her daughter ready for school on Friday. A woman played with her preschool children on Friday and looked forward to putting them down for a nap on Saturday. The man whose wife was working supervised his boys in carrying out household chores, and a woman watched TV with a neighbor's child. Children were not much mentioned, either because they are taken as a given or because the proportion of children in Millfield of school age is somewhat low.

Now we come to a crucial question. We have seen that time for Millfield residents on the day before and the day of their interviews is divided between Millfield and areas outside, mostly but not entirely greater Brixton. We have seen that within Millfield they spent considerable time working around their houses and also at leisure with their families. Less frequently they mentioned their children. But none of these were neighborly or community activities. So the crucial question is, compared with general recollection of past encounters, how much did they encounter their neighbors and how much were they involved in community activities on those two specific days? Members of four households mentioned such activities on Friday. Members of eight households mentioned such activities on Saturday.

The legendary post office did play a role. Five people perambulated the community, four of them walking, three of them specifically going to the post office. But only one referred to the post office in the way it had been described as a community center. She talked to three or four people at the post office, to one about the sociologist coming to interview. The other two mentioned going to the post office, but no encounter occurred that was specifically mentioned. A fourth was planning to take her baby for a stroll, so encounters had not yet occurred. A fifth went running. If he started from home he would have run through part of the village, then outside. In any event, his encounters would have had to be brief.

Neighborly relations were mentioned in four cases, though one of the encounters was not with a neighbor but with a son-in-law, probably from outside Millfield, who stopped out in front of the house as the interviewer arrived. One woman, the gardener trying to raise spinach, "saw several people" while she worked in the garden. Another woman, as mentioned, watched TV cartoons with a neighbor's child. And the fourth encounter was the only one approaching PG rating in any of the Millfield transcripts: "The gal next door called and she's going to a wedding this morning and she wanted to wear my black underwear." Not a request one would make of a "Hi, howyadoin'" acquaintance.

Of the other three encounters, two concerned a community event, one a meeting place. There had been an auction on one of the two Saturdays on which the interviews took place, and two went to that. One just mentioned it in passing, the other saw it as the kind of event that brings people together: "All the neighbors were there, I see a lot of people at the sale." "Was this the big event of the day?" "Oh yes! An auction in Millfield is really a big event. And all the neighbors come out. Some of 'em are there to buy, some of 'em are there to visit." The meeting place was the garage of the drag racer. Old buddies came and visited him at the shop Friday night. Asked if that was a gathering place, his father replied, "Yeah, it sure is for the...younger people. Uh-huh." This is one case in which a specific activity identified a general activity that had not been recalled in general discussion.

Image and Activity

It is easier to observe events than nonevents. But if you compare the activities to the images, one interesting aspect is the events that did not occur. Those who said people did not help one another as much as they used to may be right: No one mentioned helping anyone else within Millfield, including those who said helping had declined, though one couple was preparing for a future community event. No one mentioned watching strangers, not even the visiting sociologists. None of us, even the two with strange accents (eastern) and beards, were questioned, but it is probable that the village network had already identified us. Two were sick, but no one showed up with chicken soup. One watched a child.

Despite the perception of the couple working on their house that many newcomers were doing the same thing, only one other person was on this particular weekend. Nor was there much restoration activity visible on the two beautiful Saturdays. (Too beautiful to repair the roof? Should we have gone back on a rainy Saturday?) It may be that Millfield, as compared with gentrifying districts in the inner city, is less involved with house renovation.

The comparison of activities to image did provide some answers to some questions casually asked in Chapter I. Millfielders do work outside the village for the most part, though we can't tell much about the relation of location to the jobs. No one said he lived in Millfield because of easy access to work.

On the weekend in question, Millfielders were not involved with movies, libraries, theaters, antique shops, or department stores. Some presumably shopped in supermarkets and one couple was involved with a club. Several Millfielders went to restaurants. Some gardened, but no one mentioned playing golf. Two were involved in church activities, none in volunteer school work or the League of Women Voters.

The image of Millfield as a place to relax was confirmed. People did spend time doing nothing. And in no interview was there any sign of impatience or hurry to get on to something else. No one left early to go somewhere else.

As indicated, references to encounters with neighbors either at the post office or over the back fence (there aren't many fences in Millfield) were not much mentioned.

The auction was a central activity on one of the Saturdays. Only two mentioned attending, one with enthusiasm. Whoever she encountered didn't happen to be interviewed, or didn't think the encounter worth mentioning.

Overall, compared with the general perception of community and neighborliness in Millfield, there seemed to be a paucity of neighborly and communal relations on the two days most recent in the memories of the Millfielders reviewed. It could be that the phrasing of the question, stressing activities, caused people to think about actions rather than relationships. Or it could be, as the hypothesis suggested, that the image of neighborly encounters exceeds the reality. People like to think of themselves as having a community spirit, but their work, shopping, demands of kinship, work around the house, and need for time to relax all take precedent over the need for neighborly relations and communal activities.

Does a little go a long way? Perhaps the relationships are warm and unforced. People are generous when they are called upon, and the feeling that they can be called upon is more important than the calling. Is the appearance of Millfield, and the community it implies, more important than the frequent experiencing of that community? Perhaps the infrequency of encounters is an illustration of the lack of community pressure that makes Millfield attractive, even more attractive than the small town or village in which outside resources are less available, and people must rely on others to meet their needs.

The hypothesis, then, was confirmed in part, refuted in part. Contrary to our expectations, the urban villagers of Millfield did spend as much time in the community as they did in outside areas. But, as we expected, they gave their time to work, to shopping, to visiting family, and to the demands of ordinary work around the house. Encountering neighbors was not frequently mentioned, nor did they help look after one another, and they worked very little at improving their houses. Contrary to our expectation, a number of Millfielders did report experiencing some peace and tranquility. Millfield, on the weekend, appeared to be a place to rest, carry out domestic chores, and a jumping-off point for activity. Social interaction with neighbors was infrequent and usually causal in nature. Weekends were not filled with communal involvement.

Chapter V

Neighbors and Family

Let us assume that Millfielders spend more time on activities than they do interacting with neighbors. Still, it may be that all of us spend more time on activities than interacting. Suppose we consider the interacting as separate from activity. With whom do Millfielders interact? In so far as their interactions relate to neighbors, do they interact with some more than others? Does a community as small as Millfield have identifiable neighborhoods, or is it one big neighborhood itself? If the post office plays the role Millfielders think it does, and they walk for their mail, it could be possible that their acquaintances depend more on ambulation than propinquity. That certainly would seem to promote general acquaintance across the community. Then, to what extent do Millfielders interact with neighbors as compared to friends and family? Or are the neighbors friends and family?

Our expectation was that even in a community of sixty houses, neighborhoods would be perceived. And we expected that Millfielders would interact more with friends and family than with neighbors. Just as the community provides a comfortable base from which to carry out activities, so we expected it to form a social base. We expected to find neighbors greeted, but deeper interactions to occur with friends and family members. It would follow then that for the most part, neighbors would be different people from friends and family.

Types

We asked whether respondents thought a particular type of person lived in Millfield, whether there were cliques in the village, and then some questions about neighborhood and community.

The question on types brought forth an economic response more frequently than any other. "They don't have some of the money like people in Coopertown do." It is "not adaptive to upper-middle class environment. It is just more or less middle-middle class people." "I know this area don't have [expensive] houses like you would in Coopertown." "One common thing would be lack of money."

Three people referred directly to friendliness. "Most are pretty friendly." "Friendly, get along well with just about everyone." "Most are real friendly type people and get along with each other." And three others referred to a "just folks" characteristic that implied friendliness. "They're just good, decent people." "People more set in their life-styles...very happy and content with things the way they are." "I would say they're plain, down-to-earth folks."

But not intrusive. "Mind their own business." "You mind your own business and abide by the law and nothing happens. We get along fine." A teenage visitor thought this quality might be overdone. "Everybody's with theirself. They're not as...outgoing as down south, where I lived."

Two remarked on the percentage of older people. "Older, I would say...there's really a lot of older couples that live here." "I do enjoy very much the older population of Millfield and they seem to be an example of an old-fashioned Ohio small town that you don't see very often."

Three noted a feeling for the country town. "Then you have your own gardens and your own fruit trees." "You are not harassed with city politics day in and day out." "Nearly everybody around here has gardens." "There's something like you own part of it, part of the town...It's yours, and you don't want people abusing it."

Not everybody agreed there was a Millfield type. "Their personalities all differ pretty much." "No, I can't put 'em in one clump. They're different." But the preponderant opinion, however, seemed to be that there was a type: middle income, friendly, down to earth, laid back, fond of the village environment.

Cliques

Asking about cliques, of course, can be divisive. With only sixty households, can Millfield be anything but a community? It turned out that twelve of the households identified cliques, and only five perceived overall unity, though two of these also identified cliques. The most frequent identification related to areas within the village, though divisions were also made by interest, age, and, in one case, family.

Four regions were identified: north and south Millfield, divided by, of all things, the hardly used railroad tracks. Hickory Street was also identified both by residents and nonresidents, and on one occasion, Fioreta Lane. "I think that there are just natural groups that happen because we are neighbors. People on this side of the tracks have all known each other pretty well." "There are neighborhoods definitely. This area right here is very separated from across the railroad tracks. I know very few people there, and I know about everybody here." In kidding, those who live in north Millfield say to those who live in south Millfield, "Yeah, I live in the better part of Millfield." "Well, we always think of people down on Hickory Street as kind of dividing it, is that what you mean?" "I've always considered Hickory Street to be a neighborhood in itself and I guess those little alleys that run in between (Fioreta Lane) are another area." North Millfield but not Fioreta Lane was considered to be a neighborhood by the one resident interviewed who lived on the corner of Fioreta and Millfield.

Sometimes age was a factor. "There may be the clique of the older retired men. When the Farmer's Grill was here, a lot of the old men would go and hang out together for breakfast and coffee." "The only thing, and I'm not sayin' this to be detrimental or anything, but, uh, the children, and I'm speakin' not necessarily of my boys or anything, but I think that they kinda split apart, uh, Hickory Street. Those kids are close together because they all live right there on one street. Uh, whereas up here, at one special time, there really wasn't that many kids all the same age, see what I'm sayin'?" While on Hickory Street, they said, "When we came here there was a group of children that lived up there and did not come down here to play so much. These children played in this area and they played up there." And in the one situation in which parents and children lived next door, the daughter-in-law remarked, "I guess we are kinda 'cause we're related."

In repeating what Millfielders said about cliques and some other aspects of the community and family relations, we shall sometimes repeat comments used in the previous chapter. We hope the reader will forgive the repetition, because we think the same statement sometimes has a different meaning in a different context. Take the local Historical Society, perceived as a clique rather than a component of the community. One member of that group, for instance, said there were no cliques "unless you consider the members of the historic group that's better than anyone else, I hope nobody thinks that." Another resident associated the society with location, noting that the group "at this end tends to associate more, and there are older homes in this area, ya know…"

While some struggled to be even-handed in delineating groups, others did intend to be critical of appearances, of the young, and even of the Historical Society. Hickory Street "was beautiful down there when I lived down there. It's run down since…" "The other end of town, especially where there is vandalism and children, their children have the run of the backyards." "We have some out here thinks they're better than others, you know, but you find that in any community. Especially the young." "There's a clique of hoods," a teenager remarked. "I never thought about the kids," her mother replied, amiably, "that's true."

As for the Historical Society, recall two quotations mentioned previously. "The newer people that's got in...they're trying to change it to a, what is it?" a man asked his wife. "Historical," she prompted. "Historical thing now," he said. (You need to hear the tape to appreciate that one.) Another commented, "Just that little club they have. And not everybody is in it, so. They don't do a whole lot."

Residents of six of the households felt either that there were no cliques or that unity was the more striking aspect of the village. The lady who referred to vandalism at the other end of the village also noted that "you will find people that know everybody in town." And the man who kidded those who lived on the other side of the tracks concluded that "it's all the same really." Another specifically denied the significance of the tracks. "There's nobody lives on one side of the railroad tracks and we live on the other, or nothing like that...When you say you live in Millfield, you live in Millfield." Another saw the Historical Society not as a clique but as taking in everyone. Two women from different parts of the village in different ways seemed to associate cliques with visiting neighbors, but concluded the overall community was dominant. One said she wasn't aware of any cliques and added, "I know all my neighbors and they know me but we don't exchange and go to their house for coffee and all that kind of thing." The other, when asked about cliques, replied, "Doesn't seem to be, that's what's so nice about it. Some people visit with each other more than others, but it seems like they all go together."

There may have been a suggestion in these comments that cliques involve some intense common interest and that neighborly or community relations in Millfield were casual, rather than intense.

One Big Neighborhood

One of the authors was sitting at his upstairs window in an inner suburb of Brixton, as the first draft of this section was begun. The suburb has a population of about ten thousand. The block he lives on contains twenty houses and there are twenty-three such blocks between the avenues running north and south, before they are interrupted by avenues running east and west. There are 460 houses in that area—you couldn't call it a neighborhood or community. He knows the names of the families in the four houses directly across, and of those on each side. Another family about two-thirds of the way down the block is known because the husband works for the same organization as the author. And he knows the man on the far corner because they occasionally take the same bus. A few others are nodding acquaintances, but names are not known. So after living on the block for more than a decade, he knows the names and faces of members of eight of twenty families: 40 percent.

Now, Millfield contains about sixty houses. Would Millfielders recognize someone from twenty-four (40 percent) of the houses? That would be an awful lot of people to know. Another part of our data, (Table VI-8) shows that no person or household group in our sample could identify even half the families living in Millfield. Yet there certainly was a widely held perception, even by those who identified cliques, that Millfield was "one big neighborhood."

Asked if Millfield had neighborhoods or was one big neighborhood, ten answered flatly that it was one big neighborhood. And a substantial majority indicated they perceived the village was a community in which everyone recognized others who were residents of the village, and particularly en route to and from the post office (a center for communicating with the rest of the world), all were on nodding, smiling, greeting, stop-and-chat-for-a-moment terms.

"You walk down to the post office and meet other people." "If they happen to come by going to the post office and we're out there in front, they stop...just visit for a little while." "In the summertime, if I'm out in the yard...they'll come over and talk to me before they go in the post office." The postmaster "broadcasts what everybody's doing and really I think that is a big factor probably in the way we know each other." "I don't feel uncomfortable walking up to my friends across from the post office to visit with them social-wise. I don't feel unwelcome in any way."

The neighborhood of the whole was manifested for some on special occasions that brought people together. "Any kind of fire or anything. A train derailment. These kinds of things bring us together." A woman who had been to the house furniture auction that day said, "All the neighbors were there, I see a lot of people at the sale." "Big event of the day?" asked the interviewer. "Oh yes! An auction in Millfield is really a big event. And all the neighbors come out. Some of 'em are there to buy, some of 'em are there to visit."

There was some difference about the heterogeneity of the big neighborhood. One relatively new couple thought there was "a real mix of people." Another who had lived in Millfield longer thought the newcomers "blend with the old-timers here." Others saw more unity than blend. A long-time resident who knew a lot of people thought "everybody 'bout knows everybody." "One big family," said another. And surely the "bandwagon" perception bears repeating: "If somebody was to get on a bandwagon and say, 'all right everybody in Millfield, ya know, we're gonna have to push a lead ball from here to Brixton,' that everybody'd take their turn at pushin' it."

Two ways in which the overall concept of one big neighborhood was reflected were in the perception that Millfield was a very safe place and that people in Millfield were willing to help one another.

We have already introduced the man who illustrated the neighborhood security system by pointing to a stranger getting out of his car. "I figure a guy's out looking like that, especially if they're in old cars like that, they're looking for something to steal," and his wife explaining that if any newcomer were to "start 'hot-rodding' up and down that street, why some of us would get together and try to put a stop to it very quickly." And the woman who said that when her husband and sons were away at night, "with the neighbors right here, I feel it's a very safe place." Another remarked that no neighborhood watch was needed in Millfield. Safety was also supported by community honesty, as reflected in the story of a vegetable man, told independently by two different residents. He left a box for money and found that he had taken in more than he would if he had been there, "because residents left bills when they didn't have change." "It's still the atmosphere in this area," another man remarked, "that we could go and leave the front door open...and come back and everything's still gonna be here."

Looking out for one another also implies helping. Families help each other in sickness or death. When the man across the street died, a woman says she called all the neighbors and they brought food in. "If someone is sick, people will show up with chicken soup." And they look after children, pets, and things. When neighbors are away, one couple feeds the dog. The neighbors, in turn, feed their chickens. "We keep an eye out for each other." We have met the woman who takes care of "other people's kids just for the enjoyment of keepin' the kids around." And the men who help one another. "If he needs me, I'll let my stuff go and go down and help him. It works the same with him for me." Another thought it typical to borrow and lend tools, look after each other's "stuff." Several referred to helping one another out. "Everybody in this neighborhood helps everybody out."

The perception of one big neighborhood, however, was limited in a number of ways. Residents pointed out that visiting was restricted by certain norms and that friendliness could go with minding one's business. Few claimed close friends in the community and it was apparent that some of the descriptions of a community neighborhood actually applied to a much more limited neighborhood. Finally, some people thought mutual helping may be declining.

The descriptions of friendly interaction tended to be outdoor activities. "People walk around and say 'Hi' and maybe go up on the porch to talk for ten minutes." On the porch, but not in the house. As another explained, children go into other peoples' houses, but not adults. While they may talk to neighbors frequently, "we don't play cards with anybody or anything like that." Another said they talk and help one another out but "don't visit." "And they meet ya, and ya laugh and talk...Even if they're going some place, they'll talk to ya a few minutes before they leave. Holler at ya, and if you're on the porch they're always wavin' or blowin' a horn at ya or somethin'."

Perhaps such friendly relations exist because they are not completely open. One can laugh and joke if one does not probe. And there were lots of comments that suggested such limitations were desirable. "I don't know why I should talk about (the neighbors)," said one older lady. "I don't know them. Don't mess with them." Yet she also described how she helped them in time of illness and looked forward to people stopping by as they went to or from the post office. Another long-time resident said he doesn't have much to do with the neighbors, but does talk to them, help them, lend to them, and look after their "stuff." He thought that was typical. While he looked after stuff, his wife looked after children. Another said Millfielders look after things, help when there is a problem, "but we don't associate, you know." He also thought that was typical. Possibly the best summary of this attitude was "I mean, they don't care, but they, uh, they do care, but they're not pushy in the caring." And then there was the man commenting on the beauty of the community and its foliage, who concluded, "you can sit in your yard and not even see your neighbors."

One resident, who had a close friend in Millfield, thought that most people get to know one another, but close friendships are not common. Her neighbor was close enough to borrow her black underwear that day. A nearby resident said he and his wife visit the house of only one neighbor, though they talk to several. Another had a close outdoor relation with his neighbor, who was highly regarded by his younger son because of his abilities with cars and motorcycles. A son and daughter, age twenty-two and eighteen, respectively, said the neighbor's sons and daughters of the same sex were best friends.

Even when people were describing Millfield as one big neighborhood, their examples suggested more limited contacts. One woman commented that she sees neighbors "especially in the summer, about every day because we share a driveway, and I go over and talk to them, you know." We have already met the walnut neighbors. A younger man described where he lived as "more of a neighborhood full of kids." "Oh, that's true," agreed his wife. An older woman who had moved within Millfield referred to the house she had lived in as her "old neighborhood." When people were asked to describe on a map where others lived, they usually did much better with the houses nearby. One couple felt others had lots of friends in the community as whole, but they didn't because they lived at one end of the village. Asked where they met others, members of eight households said, "while working in the yard." "Summer, when you are out," said one, "you're always talking to neighbors right around."

So many of the specifics seem related to neighbors living next door or across the street rather than to the community as a whole.

The idea that everyone helps everyone was presented by several people as a Millfield universal, more common than visiting or socializing. But even here some had reservations. One younger woman didn't think older women helped much because they worked. An older man thought, "maybe several of us (help one another) more than the majority." Another older man thought people didn't help one another as much as they used to. And one grumbled, "I don't get much help." When asked about their activities on the day before and the day of the interview, no one in any of the households interviewed gave any indication of having helped or been helped by a neighbor.

So one big neighborhood may exist precisely because it doesn't make too many demands. People are friendly but not probing, will help when needed, are trustworthy. But they do not lay heavy obligations on one another. It would appear, however, that Millfielders retain the image of one big neighborhood at the same time that they delineate neighborhoods. The separation of Hickory Street from Millfield Road was perceived by residents of both streets. When specific interactions were described, they more frequently concerned neighbors living nearby. We shall explore some aspects of these distinctions between neighborhood and community in the next chapter.

Group Memberships

Millfielders, like most Americans, had various group memberships, more outside Millfield than in. A few seemed to be deeply involved, but most were not.

Members of eight households mentioned belonging to the Millfield Historical Society, and another couple felt they should belong because they do have interest in local historical preservation. At least half a dozen seemed to have considerable involvement. One who was now less active mentioned being a founder. Two were on the Board of Directors, and one knew all the members of the Board. One put out a newsletter and one was astonished that everyone in Millfield didn't know about the society. It seemed there was a level of commitment and the society was well established, but it was one of many activities in busy lives.

Five households had members in service organizations outside Millfield, but only one of these couples seemed to be deeply involved, spending the previous evening at the VFW, helping put up a flagpole the morning of the interview, and preparing to spend several hours at the headquarters making a dinner. They also belonged to the Military Order of the Cooties within the VFW and had built a float for parades, which gave a unique aspect to their backyard.

Two women in the community were involved in church activities outside Millfield to the extent that on Saturday they were studying material they were going to present to children the next day. Members of six households mentioned belonging to churches outside Millfield and two were members of the one church located within the community.

One woman was seriously involved with Shaklee, a group concerned with dietary health. She attended meetings once a week. "You're not familiar with Shaklee?" she asked the interviewer. "I can't believe this!"

One man was even more deeply involved in outside athletic activities. He had been a baseball, football, and basketball coach for the past decade. He used to play on a softball team that played 125 games a year and he took his wife and children to the games. He had worked twenty-five years as an announcer and events director at the Coopertown Drag Strip and is an announcer at another more distant drag strip. He was the most deeply involved of all Millfielders in outside activities and on the day of the interview was supervising his children while his wife worked. Yet his was the longest of all the interviews.

Other outside activities did not seem to play a major role. One family belonged to the county historical society. One belonged to the Millfield Alumni, a group of older residents that was mentioned by no other family. Three mentioned professional activities, two of those being involved in the American Business Woman's Association. And one mentioned belonging to no groups. "I never did go in for stuff like that. Bars and partyin' and stuff like that."

A number mentioned organized group activities within Millfield, most of them apparently planned by the Millfield Society. The interviews were conducted in October and six persons mentioned the upcoming Halloween party. Nine mentioned the annual community picnic. "And when they have the community picnic everybody really enjoys themselves and makes a casserole of some kind, baked goods, and they always have contests for the children. So the younger people take an interest in it also." One also mentioned a yearly fish fry that apparently was for Hickory Street only. Six mentioned yard or garage sales and four mentioned a yearly clean up, but without the enthusiasm expressed for Halloween and the picnic.

Several mentioned not participating in any of these community activities. One was out of town so much. Another thought they cost too much "and boy, when you got a limited income, you gotta watch what you're doing." "I got so many other interests." "I should (participate) because I am one of the older residents but I never got into things like that." Concerning activities as a whole, residents of thirteen households spoke favorably about them, seven had reservations. But even though that would suggest that a majority of Millfielders do participate in such activities, still the planning would not have to be very extensive, and there appear to be only four major events a year. So while they renew a sense of community, they do not involve a great deal of commitment.

Several mentioned activities with friends outside of organized groups. On the weekends of the interviews, four unmarried younger people mentioned activities with friends, drinking beer at a Coopertown pub, going to a football game, or congregating in the Millfield garage. Among older people, two mentioned having coffee with friends at the nearest Coopertown restaurant on Friday night. One mentioned going trapshooting with friends, and one older couple mentioned visiting the wife's friend outside the greater Brixton area. Another said that he was going to work on a lady's car, but that she had promised him a dinner. So that makes members of nine households engaged in activities with friends in a single weekend, suggesting that friends do constitute an important part of leisure encounters. But outside of activities, little was said about friends. Perhaps they were taken for granted or perhaps the questions were framed in such a way that they were not perceived as relevant.

Alone

Before turning to relations and activities with family and kin, it should be noted that even in a warm and friendly community, people spend a lot of time alone. Asked about activities on a Friday and Saturday, the following were noted: Six mentioned commercial exchanges—shopping for groceries, leaving or collecting dry cleaning, buying baby or maternity clothes, stopping at the bank, leaving a motor for servicing. Twelve men mentioned working outside in their yards, or on the outside of their houses, trying out a new tiller, cutting the lawn, working on cars, feeding ducks. One man mentioned professional yard work outside Millfield. In ten houses people were doing housework or cooking, including laundry, housecleaning, fixing a cabinet door, scrubbing the kitchen floor, washing dishes "for the wife," making noodles. Seventeen mentioned engaging in some kind of sit down work or relaxation: reading, crocheting, watching TV, listening to the radio, sewing, doing homework, preparing Sunday school lessons, working on crafts. Six of those doing needlework or crafts were making clothes or blankets. The six TV watchers were concerned with ball games, cartoons, soaps, and the news. The readers read papers, magazines, and history books. Four mentioned extra sleeping and one mentioned taking it easy. Three mentioned grooming: showering, bathing, washing hair. Only one mentioned jogging.

It is a minor point, but in considering social activities, one should note that there is much that we do by ourselves, even though others are around us. We shop while others shop, work in the yard while our spouse works in the house, or work in different rooms. In one household a husband tried out a new tiller and did odds and ends around the house while his son cut the lawn and did his homework and his wife cleaned a bedroom, did the laundry, read the paper, and watched the news. In another household a husband described evenings with his wife: "She likes crafts and I like reading about history so she'll work on her crafts here and I will be reading out in the kitchen."

To be alone is not to be lonely.

The Nuclear Family

The most frequently mentioned family activities involved married couples. Half the households mentioned sharing outside entertainment: going to restaurants, fishing, going to a retirement dinner, taking trips, going to fairs, Sunday driving, going to ball games, camping, movies. "We do everything together," said one older woman. "We don't get two feet away from each other," said her husband. "We like to fish and we like to...eat out and we like the VFW, of course, and we like to take trips," she said. "We like fairs," he added. "We went up to the Brown Jug and horse races, watched trotters and pacers." Another older couple was going to a distant city to a retirement party the night of the interview, then back the next day to a ball game. "Oh, yeah. We do about everything together."

Shopping together was mentioned rarely. Couples might go to a garage sale together looking for a specific household item or make a purchase while out for other reasons. On the weekends of the interviews, one couple bought the wife a coat at a garage sale; another bought the husband a pair of shoes. No couple went grocery shopping together or mentioned ever doing it.

There were two very different family references to work outside of Millfield. The man whose wife worked Saturdays mentioned phoning her about the progress of household chores and also mentioned visiting her at work because he likes to see her in the daylight once in a while. Another couple work together at fairs. "We sell fudge and work flower beds and stuff like that, and we have stands."

Six people mentioned being home together working or relaxing: staying at home "pooped," watching TV, or spending the afternoon relaxing in the backyard. A couple were getting some things together for a community garage sale. Another couple often worked in the garden together. A third couple was about to clean out bookshelves and strip, sand, and refinish the floors. But references of this sort were rare, either because they were taken for granted or because other activities really did limit time together at home. Two made comments that suggested the latter possibility. "What little free time we have, we try to do things together. We could be more successful at that, it's an objective." "We live our different lives really to a large extent. About the only thing we do together is the house, working on it. We both work, so on the weekend I'm doing the house and he's doing the cars. We switch off cutting the grass."

Activities with children were mentioned in ten of the twelve households that had children. Children were being watched, engaging in normal home activities, playing, working, or going somewhere.

The home activities tended to be routine, briefly described. One mentioned playing with children, two putting them to bed, one having family dinners (though her older children were rarely home at the same time). One man was supervising his children at chores, and a woman was working with her visiting mother and sister in the yard, so you could say a mother was working with her children.

Activities with children outside Millfield seemed more interesting and varied. On the weekend of the interview one family was taking their baby to walk the streets and glens of a nearby college town. An older father was going to watch his son in the drag races. Others reported that they engaged in such activities at one time or had in the past: One family worked on the farm where the parents hope to retire; another reported that they see plays once in a while and go to church together. The mother added that "when you kids were young we went camping and things like that." But now they do their own thing.

Some adults took children various places. A mother took her daughter to a skating lesson and another child to the doctor. A woman and her older son went to the bank and grocery shopping. A man took his son to football practice in Coopertown. It had gotten easier, though, he thought. A few years earlier his wife would often be taking one child to play at one place while he'd be taking another to play elsewhere.

In all, few nuclear family activities were mentioned. We have gathered here all those specifically mentioned as taking place on the weekend of the interview, and those mentioned taking place at other times.

Relatives

As anticipated, Millfielders usually have relatives in the greater Brixton area or within an hour's drive. Residents of nineteen of the twenty-four households reported relatives within that range. There were parents, children, grandchildren, cousins, uncles, aunts, nieces, nephews, and three generations of in-laws.

Only three households had relatives living in Millfield. Two of them were parents and children of the same family, both interviewed. A third was a niece, daughter of a wife's sister's former husband. Only three households reported relatives living out of state, and only one specifically mentioned having no relative within an hour of Millfield.

The litany of these relatives in the area may sound like a page from Genesis, but like that book it has something of a ring to it. Parents in Brixton, cousins, an aunt and uncle in the greater Brixton area. Three brothers in Brixton, daughters in Corinth and Coopertown. Six grandchildren and four great grandchildren, all boys. "We got both my daughters and his daughter. We got cousins and what have you." A mother in Coopertown and son in Brixton, four living sisters, one living with her mother. Both sets of parents and brothers and sisters within an hour's drive. Both parents on each side in Brixton and she has a brother and sister in Corinth, he a sister in another Brixton suburb. A brother in Coopertown and three sisters each living a mile away in different directions. Unspecified relatives in Corinth. "Mother-in-law, father-in-law, a couple of others, my dad." Two brothers in Brixton, mother and aunt in Corinth. Mother and two sisters in Brixton. Daughter-in-law and sister-in-law in Coopertown. Brother-in-law in Brixton. Cousin in Coopertown, a son of hers and a son of theirs in Brixton. Two brothers, two sisters, and another unmarried sister living with mother. Daughter, mother-in-law, and brother-in-law in Brixton. Two brothers and a sister in greater Brixton. Uncles and aunts in Brixton. An exploration of those relationships suggests that some families are split up, or perhaps some relatives forgotten.

How often were relatives visited? Thirteen mentioned seeing relatives at least once a week. Members of four households said once a month, and in nine households visitation occurred less than once a month. Those most frequently visited appear to be parents, then siblings. One reason that children were less frequently visited may be that only ten families were old enough to have children living away from home, while in eighteen of the families the oldest member was under sixty, young enough for the probability of at least one surviving parent. Of those who visited less than once a month, two had children in the Far West. Of the others, two mentioned siblings visited less than once a month, and none mentioned parents.

The nature of the visits varied. A number mentioned visiting relatives in the greater Brixton area the weekend of the interview. One had visited her sister-in-law in Corinth. Another helped his brother-in-law paint a frame cabin in a town outside the Brixton area. A couple had gone to her cousin's house to play cards. A daughter had visited her grandmother. A young man was going to help his brother-in-law move furniture. A man cut wood for his daughter who lived in Coopertown. A man was going to watch his grandson play Pee Wee football in Corinth. Another mentioned that his son was working on his uncle's "terrific H. O. gauge train." On a longer range, one woman had just arrived with her sister and brother-in-law from Las Vegas after visiting children who had come up from Arizona. On a shorter range a man was talking to his son-in-law in the driveway when the interviewer arrived. A cousin's car was parked in the driveway while the cousin attended the local auction.

Others mentioned kinds of contacts they had outside of the current weekend. One man mentioned that his father had had a series of strokes and his mother's health was poor so "I make it a point to go up there at least once a week." Another said her sister-in-law (i.e., her husband's sister) drives her husband to work and that she does her laundry at her mother-in-law's house. A man mentioned that he and his brother both work for the same company, so they see each other daily. And a man worked in the same place as his son. He and his wife played cards at her cousin's house weekly, as indeed they had done the night before. The families living next door, parents and children, said they often went fishing together, joined by Uncle Phil, the mother's brother. This uncle, his Millfield brother, and their Millfield father also often hunted together.

Within Millfield, "Mom and Dad from the city like to come out and just sit on the swing and watch the cars go by and stuff, ya know. Because it's more leisurely...they just come out and enjoy themselves." An older woman's daughter "comes out every Wednesday and we go shopping." The daughter's husband and her grandson "come down and mow the yard for me" (though the day before she had mowed it herself). Her daughter in Texas "is talkin' about coming in, maybe, sometime next year for a visit." A military wife, whose husband was in the Far East, was being visited for the year by her mother and younger sister. The man who works in the same place as his son said the son came every Sunday night for supper. The two families living next door, parents and son, mentioned they frequently have coffee together in the mornings and barbecues quite often.

We mentioned that one Millfield woman had just returned from visiting her children in the West. The other woman who had children in the West said she had lived with her daughter and her (daughter's) husband for a couple of years when the husband was still in the service. Then she spent a couple of winters in Arizona with them.

Findings

We expected that most families would have kin in the greater Brixton area rather than in Millfield itself and that these relatives would be encountered at least weekly. Our expectations were met, but not resoundingly. Twenty of the twenty-four households reported kin living within an hour of Millfield and thirteen of these reported encountering at least one of these relatives weekly or more frequently. There is mild support of our expectation that long-time residents would have more frequent contacts with kin from other areas. Nine of the fourteen families (64 percent) residing in Millfield longer than a decade versus 40 percent of the more recent families saw nearby kin at least on a weekly basis.

Whether family relationships are more important than community relationships is difficult to ascertain. It would appear that neighbors and the community provide a generally supportive but superficial background against which more intensive family relationships occurred.

The question of the relation between neighborhood and community will be explored more fully in the next chapter. But from the testimony of the Millfielders themselves, without detailed exploration of networks, it appears that they perceive Millfield as a single community in the sense that anyone from the community would greet anyone else on the way to the post office, as they did the visiting interviewers. The people who come up on porches, however, or linger over back fences, are likely to be neighbors. Hickory Street was perceived as a neighborhood both by those who lived there and those who did not. When others talked of interacting, borrowing, or playing walnut jokes, they were speaking of neighbors. Even membership in the historical society, it turned out, was less likely to be based on education or time of residence in the town than on living on Millfield Road. Most who spoke favorably of the society lived on or adjacent to the village's central thoroughfare. Most who had reservations about it did not.

Activities with friends, though less noted, may play an important part in the lives of the Millfielders. On the two days in which activities were reported, members of nine households mentioned some kind of outside activity with friends. Nuclear family activities mentioned were not overly conspicuous. Half the households mentioned a variety of activities, including eating out, taking trips, shopping, driving, camping, entertainment. The families also spent time together at home, resting, watching TV, working in the house or garden, supervising or playing with children, taking trips with them, and driving them to various activities in greater Brixton. These activities did not occupy a great deal of time on the two days explored, but rather seemed incidental and occasional. Perhaps they were taken for granted.

There seemed to be more zest in describing extended families. People seemed to enjoy repeating the litanies of siblings, parents, children, and in-laws living near Millfield. Visits with kin to distant relatives were obviously special occasions. Visits with kin involved joint work, games, health care, and commuter transportation. Only four families mentioned relatives visiting Millfield.

All told, Millfielders described more specific activities with friends, family, and relatives, most of it outside Millfield, while their relations with neighbors and community were more general, perhaps more frequent, but not as easy to describe. It seems that the community, with its generally supportive and mellow background, provides a setting for more intense activities and relationships that are carried out with friends and family, much of it beyond Millfield.

Chapter VI

Circles of Acquaintance

Is it redundant to refer to friends as neighbors? Wouldn't your neighbors be your friends? Not necessarily. Carol Silverman (1987) thinks that this assumption has misled some community researchers. It may be, rather, that neighbors perform some other function. The neighborhood may be a place of refuge, a comfortable area from which one may engage in more intense relationships with one's nuclear family or with friends or kin outside the community. As one Millfielder has put it, you greet your neighbors on the street, but you don't invite them into your house.

We have seen in the previous chapter that Millfielders made a distinction between friends and neighbors in their descriptions of activities. Their days were rich in specific activities with friends and family, while references to neighbors were more general. They could describe how they greeted neighbors passing the house, but they would not perceive such a greeting as an activity they would consider reporting as occurring yesterday or today.

On the other hand, some neighbors might be friends. It is often the image of the situation comedy or the soap opera that friends live next door. If neighbors interact and find themselves compatible, they might become friends over a period of time. Or it might be that friends, visiting Millfield, would find it so attractive that they would buy a house when it came up for sale.

To test this, we gave the families we interviewed a map of Millfield and asked them to identify as many individuals or families as they could who resided in these homes. Typically, the map would be set on the dining room table, and members of the family would discuss who lived where, correcting each other, debating whether it was this house or that house. It was rather fun. Figure VI-1 shows a map similar to the one they were given.

After everyone who could be had been identified, we asked the families to indicate whether any of the persons named would be one of their three best friends. Then we had them circle the houses in which these best friends lived.

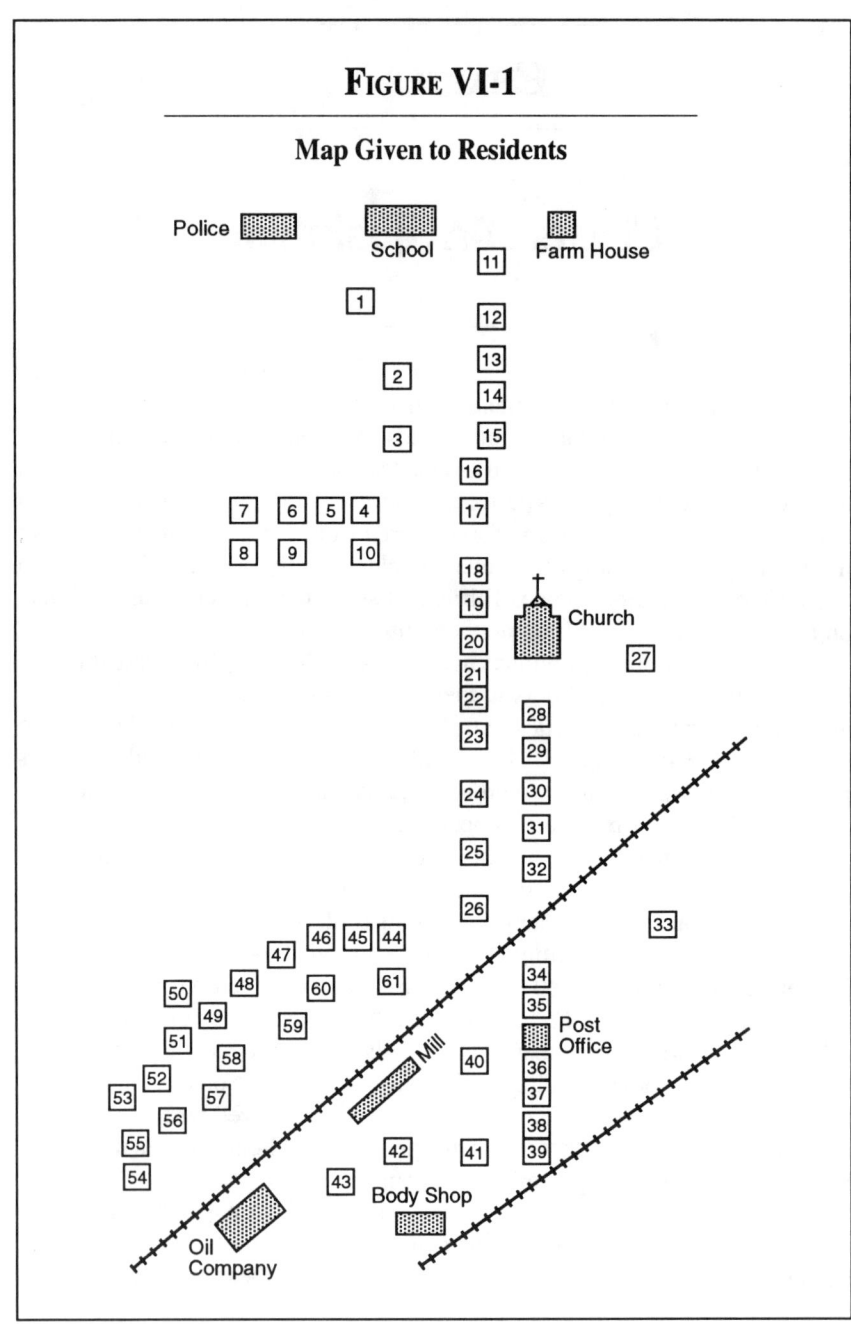

FIGURE VI-1

Map Given to Residents

Circles of Aquaintance

TABLE VI-1

Grid of Neighbors and Best Friends

[Table VI-1: A large grid showing relationships among households across three neighborhoods (North Millfield, Central Millfield, South Millfield, and Hickory Street). Rows represent sample households (numbered 1, 4, 6, 8, 10, 12, 14, 20, 24, 25, 26, 29, 35, 38, 40, 41, 42, 46, 48, 49, 51, 56) and columns represent all households (1–32). Cell entries are K = Known, F = Friend, • = Own Household. Row and column totals are provided.]

KEY
F = Friend ST = Sub Total T = Total
K = Known • = Own Household FB = Considered Friend by Others
KB = Known By

TABLE VI-1 (CONTINUED)

Grid of Neighbors and Best Friends

Neighborhoods		South Millfield											ST	Hickory Street																		ST	TK	TKB	TF	TFB
Households		33	34	35	36	37	38	39	40	41	42	43	11	44	45	46	47	48	49	50	51	52	53	54	55	56	57	58	59	60	61	18				
	1		K	K			K		K		K		5			K			K		K					K	K			K		6	24	19	2	2
North	4												0																			0	5	3	0	0
Millfield	6												0																			0	9	7	1	0
	8					K							1						K		K	K							K			4	12	9	0	1
	10								K		K		3						K		K								K			3	29	15	2	1
	12												0																			0	6	6	0	0
	14												0																			0	12	8	1	1
													9																			13				
Central	20												0						K													1	10	6	0	0
Millfield	24		K	K			K		K	K			6						K		K								K	K		4	23	13	0	2
	25						K		K				3			K		K	K		K								K	K	K	7	17	13	0	2
	26			K									1																			0	8	14	3	1
	29	K	K	K	K	K	K		K	K	K	K	10		K	K	K	K	K		K	K	K	K		K	K	K	K		K	15	52	13	1	0
													20																			27	110			
South	35	F	K	•	K	K	K		K			K	7			K		K	K									K	K	K	K	6	17	10	1	0
Millfield	38	K	K	K	K	K	•	K	K	K	K	K	10					K	K									K	K	K	K	6	41	9	0	0
	40	K	K	K		K	K		•	K	K	K	8	K	K				K		K			K	K			K	K			8	35	11	0	1
	41		K		K	K	K		F	•		K	6				K	K	K										K		K	5	25	7	1	0
	42										•	K	1																			0	6	7	0	0
													32																			25				
Hickory	46	K	K	K							K		4		F	•	F	K	K		K		K	K		K			K	K	F	11	28	7	6	0
Street	48		K	K	K	K	K		K	K			7		K	K	F	•	K	K	K	K	K	K		K	K	K	K	K	F	15	43	8	3	1
	49			K	K	K			K			K	5			K	K	F	•	F	F	K	K	K		K	K	K	K	K	K	14	35	15	6	1
	51	K		K						K		K	4		K	K	K	K	F	F	•	K	K			K	K	K	K	K	K	14	32	11	2	1
	56				K		K		K	K		K	5					K			K					•	F					3	18	6	1	0
													25																			57				
Times Known		7	9	10	7	8	9	1	11	7	7	10	86	1	5	7	6	8	15	3	11	5	5	4	1	6	6	6	13	9	10	122	487	217	30	14
Times Considered Friend		1	0	0	0	0	0	0	1	0	0	0		0	1	0	2	1	1	2	1	0	0	0	0	0	1	0	1	0	2					

Circles of Aquaintance

TABLE VI-2

Acquaintances and Best Friends of Respondents within Millfield

Neighborhood of Respondent	Neighborhood of Acquaintances and Friends														
	N. Millfield (N=17)			C. Millfield (N=15)			S. Millfield (N=11)			Hickory (N=18)					
	K	F	TK	K	F	TK	K	F	TK	K	F	TK	TK	TKB	TF	TFB
N. Millfield (N=7)	50	4	54	19	2	21	9	0	9	13	0	13	97	67	6	5
C. Millfield (N=5)	24	1	25	35	3	38	20	0	20	27	0	27	110	59	4	5
S. Millfield (N=5)	26	1	27	40	0	40	30	2	32	25	0	25	124	44	2	1
Hickory St. (N=5)	32	2	34	37	3	40	25	0	25	43	12	57	156	47	18	3
Totals	132	8	140	131	8	139	84	2	86	109	12	122	487	217	30	14

Key (Same as Table VI-1)

These two questions produced an amazing amount of data. After wrestling with it in various ways, we put it on a grid of neighbors and friends (Table VI-1). Down the left hand side of the grid are the twenty-two households who reviewed the map. Across the top are the sixty-one households of Millfield. Ks indicate people known. Someone in the household at the left was able to identify someone in the household marked K. Fs indicate best friends. Someone in the household at the top has been identified by someone in the household at the left as a best friend. Of course, Fs would also count as known.

A condensed version of Table VI-1 is presented in Table VI-2. It summarizes the number of acquaintances and friends named by all respondents residing within a given neighborhood.

Subtotals represent possible neighborhoods. While one may recommend establishing neighborhoods according to friendship or acquaintance networks, at this point we had not established a method for doing so. These candidate neighborhoods come from the Millfielders' own perceptions. These neighborhoods were not quite the same as those mentioned when Millfielders were asked if their village had neighborhoods. When looking at the maps, several Millfielders divided the area north of the tracks into north and central Millfield. This distinction was made by householders living in both areas. On the other hand, Fioretta Lane, distinguished only once in the neighborhood question, was not mentioned by anyone working on the maps. So the neighborhoods distinguished by the Millfielders reviewing the maps were north, central, and south Millfield, with a general recognition of Hickory Street as a fourth distinct area.

To better understand what Table VI-2 tells us about the location of friends and acquaintances in Millfield, let's use responses of residents in the neighborhood of north Millfield as an example. The seven "northender"

TABLE VI-3

Acquaintances by Household

	Respondent Households	Total Households	Millfield HH Could Know Millfield	Did Know Millfield	Percent Known in Millfield	Own Neighborhood Could Know Nbhd	Did Know Nbhd	Percent Known in Nbhd	Nbhd Percent Higher	Neighbors as Percent of Mlfders
Millfield (Total)	22	61	1320	487	37%					
North Millfield	7	17	420	97	23%	112	54	48%	109%	56%
Central Millfield	5	15	300	110	39%	70	38	54%	46%	35%
South Millfield	5	11	300	124	41%	50	32	64%	56%	76%
Hickory Street	5	18	300	156	52%	85	57	67%	29%	37%

respondents identified a total of fifty-four households in their own neighborhood. On the average each respondent names 7.7 other northender households. Four of these known households contain personal friends of respondents. Only twenty-one households in central Millfield, nine in south Millfield, and thirteen on Hickory Street were known to any of the respondents. Northenders knew considerably fewer Millfielders than any other neighborhood. Each respondent, on the average, named 13.8 other households compared to an average of 22.1 households for all respondents in the sample.

Given the relatively few residents of other neighborhoods known by the average northender, it is surprising that a northender is just as likely to be known by other Millfielders as residents of any other neighborhood. An average of 6.4 northender households were named by all respondents compared to 6.3, 3.9, and 5.5 households in the other three neighborhoods. So while northenders are least likely to know Millfielders in other neighborhoods, they are somewhat more likely to be known than members of certain other neighborhoods.

Who Knows Whom?

First of all, it is apparent that if everyone knows everyone at Millfield's post office, it would not be the case that everyone knows where everyone lives. A glance at the grid indicates that there are a large number of blanks where no one in a household could identify anyone from the family living in another. Table VI-3 explores the extent to which people were able to identify who lives in other houses, as a whole, and by neighborhood.

There are sixty-one houses in Millfield, so if someone in each of the twenty-two households interviewed could identify someone in every other house in Millfield, each household would identify sixty other households, their own, of course, excluded, which would mean that twenty-two times sixty, or 1320, identifications were possible. In fact, 487 identifications were made, 37 percent of the possible number.

If these identifications were examined according to the discrete areas perceived by Millfielders, would respondents be able to identify more households in their own "neighborhood" than in others? The table shows how many families looked at the maps in each neighborhood and how many households each neighborhood has. Then it shows how many households could have been identified in Millfield as a whole and how many in the home neighborhood. Percentages are calculated for Millfield as a whole and for each neighborhood.

The finding here appears decisive. In each case, the percent known in the neighborhood is considerably higher than the percent known for Millfield as a whole. It varies from Hickory Street, where a household is 9 percent more likely to identify a neighborhood to 109 percent for north Millfield. Despite the perception that Millfield is one big neighborhood, there is considerable justification for calling the sub areas, as identified by Millfielders, "neighborhoods."

It is interesting, though, that the neighborhood most spontaneously identifiable to Millfielders, the Hickory Street neighborhood, is the one that appears to be most integrated into the community, while north Millfield appears to be the least integrated. This is also surprising from the viewpoint of postal dynamics since the north Millfielders would have to walk by all the central Millfield houses to get to the post office. Perhaps it is time to put the neighborhoods into the map so that this becomes apparent (Figure VI-2).

When the twenty-two households are broken into four neighborhoods, there are not enough in any neighborhood for statistically significant comparisons. But a check of the households in north Millfield indicates average education (twelve years) an equal division between textbook and colloquial grammar, and average residence (fourteen median, seventeen mean). So there is nothing special about length of residence or education that would explain the comparative lack of community involvement suggested in north Millfield. Residents of this area knew fewer people in Millfield by household than did residents in any other area, and even though they knew more than twice as many in their own neighborhood versus the rest of the village, they knew a lower percentage even there than did members of the households interviewed in the other three neighborhoods.

Peripheral location is another possible explanation, except that south Millfield is equally peripheral, perhaps more so since it is on the other side of the tracks, and Hickory Street could be seen as peripheral in the sense that it is the only neighborhood totally separated from the main Millfield Road. South Millfield is central in the sense that the post office is there and other residents

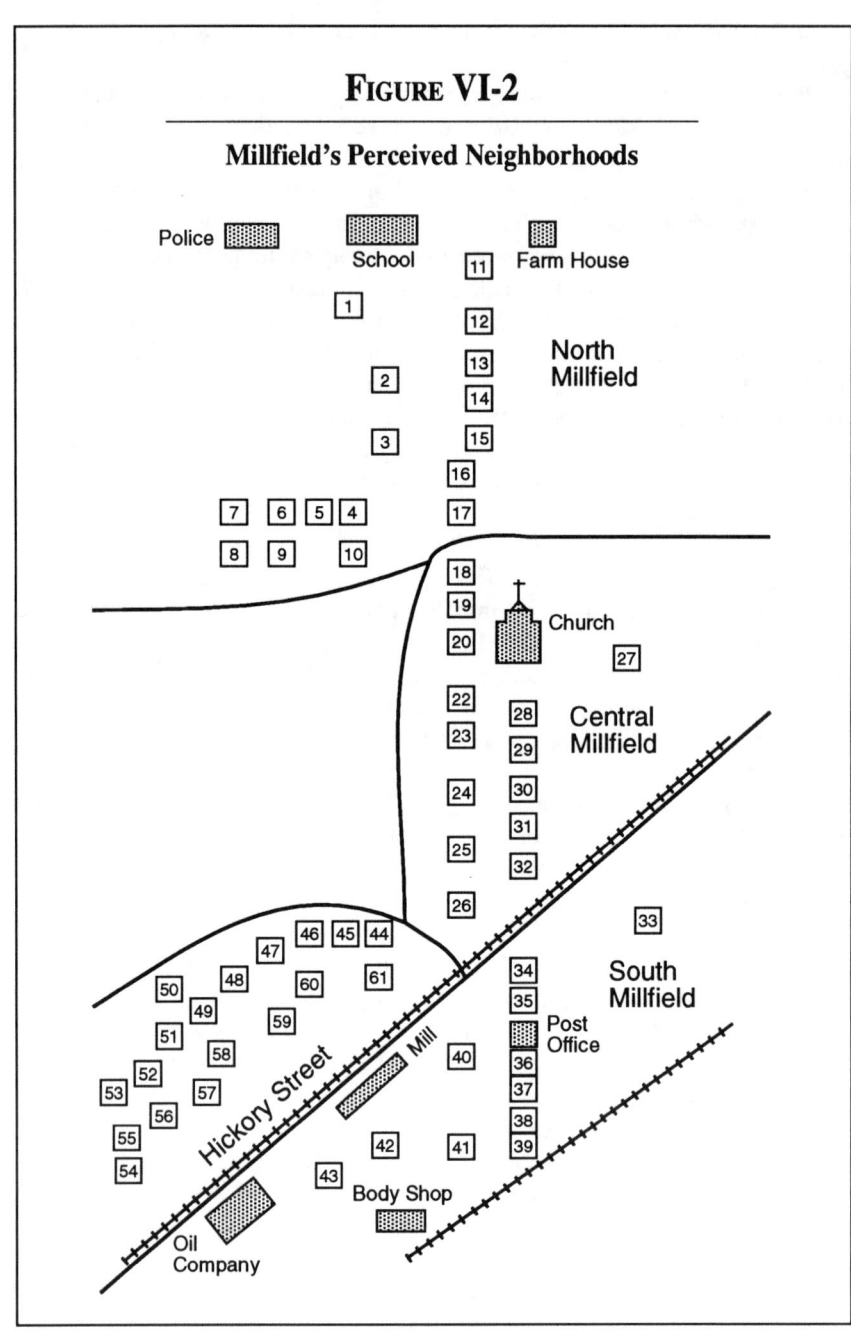

come to it. Central Millfield, clearly not peripheral in any sense, was second lowest in the percentage of households known in Millfield and in neighborhood. So location does not seem to be an explanation.

Are You Closer If You Are Closer?

Could it be that people are more likely to be acquainted simply as a function of distance? Aren't you more likely to know who lives next door or across the street than who lives in a particular house on the next block? Would it be any different in a community like Millfield?

Wondering how to answer that, we took a compass and drew 200-foot circles around a centrally located house of a long-time resident and checked to see how many households she knew and how many knew her. Then we wondered how that would compare with a long-term resident at the edge of town, so we did the same thing with his house. Then we tried it on a house on a borderline between neighborhoods. Then we added two more houses, to be sure we had one in each neighborhood, choosing residents of varying lengths, but those who knew a large number of families, say in the range of twenty to thirty-five. The drawing of the circles, by the way, showed that the two houses farthest from one another in Millfield (nos. 11 and 54) are only two-fifths of a mile apart.

Having found out the distances of households identified by each of the five households measured, we also considered the relation between distance and being known by others. This produced smaller numbers, since we could only consider the other households that had been sampled. But as an additional check we added together the known and being known columns as a measure of the relationship between distance and reciprocal relationship.

The map in Figure VI-3 shows the five households (shaded) tested in this way, and 200-foot concentric circles drawn around the central Millfield house. The houses numbered are those identified by the occupant of house 24. (It happened that she knew someone in each of the other four houses tested.) There are maps, not shown, for each of these other four houses that are similar to Figure VI-3.

Table VI-4 shows the relation between acquaintance and distance by three measures: known, known by, and known plus known by.

As Table VI-4 shows, for the five households, the percentage of households identified dropped for each 200 feet distance until 1000 feet was reached. Beyond 1000 feet, the distance factor no longer applied, or rather, was reversed, so that the same percentage was identified beyond 1200 feet as had been identified between 600 and 800 feet.

84 Millfield on Saturday: Searching for Community in a Metropolitan Village

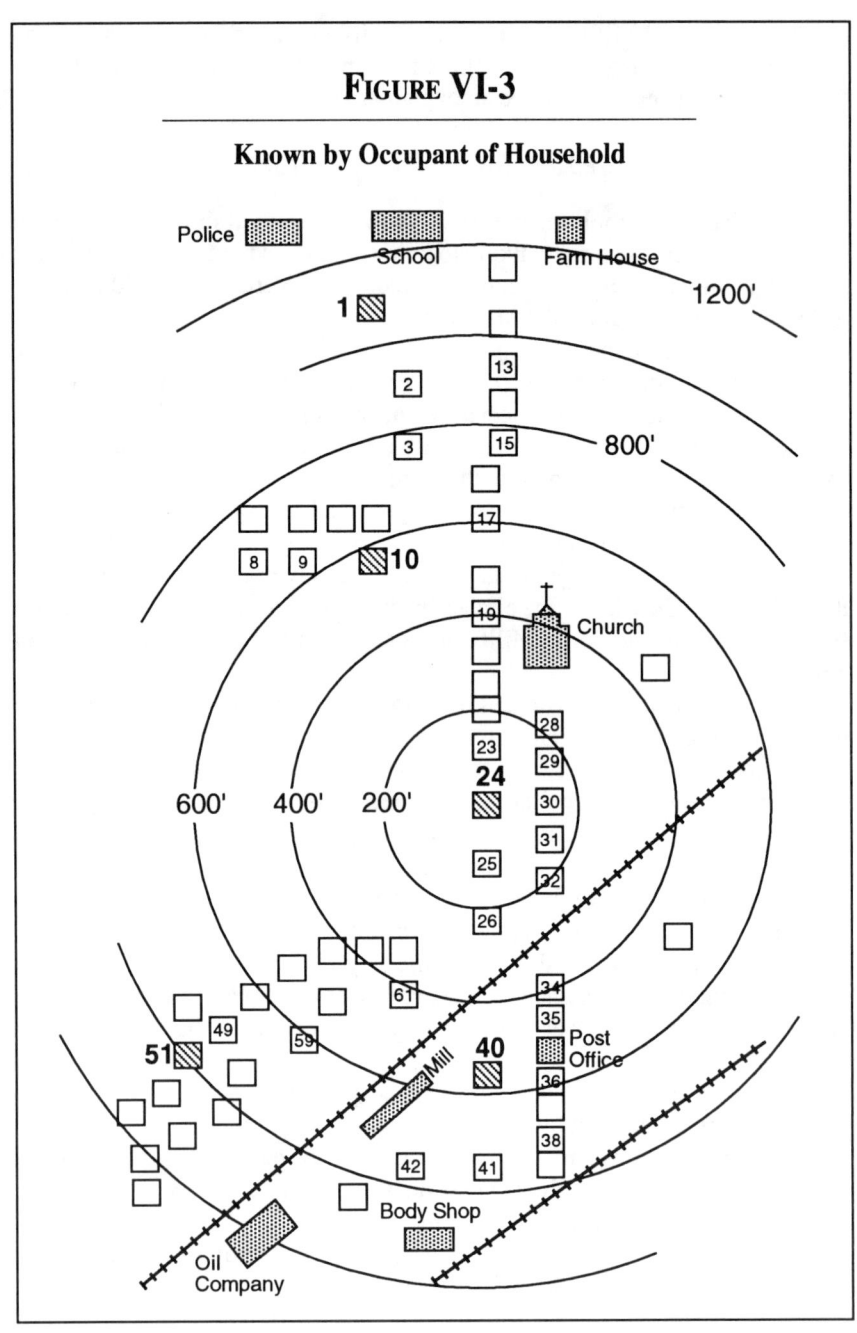

FIGURE VI-3

Known by Occupant of Household

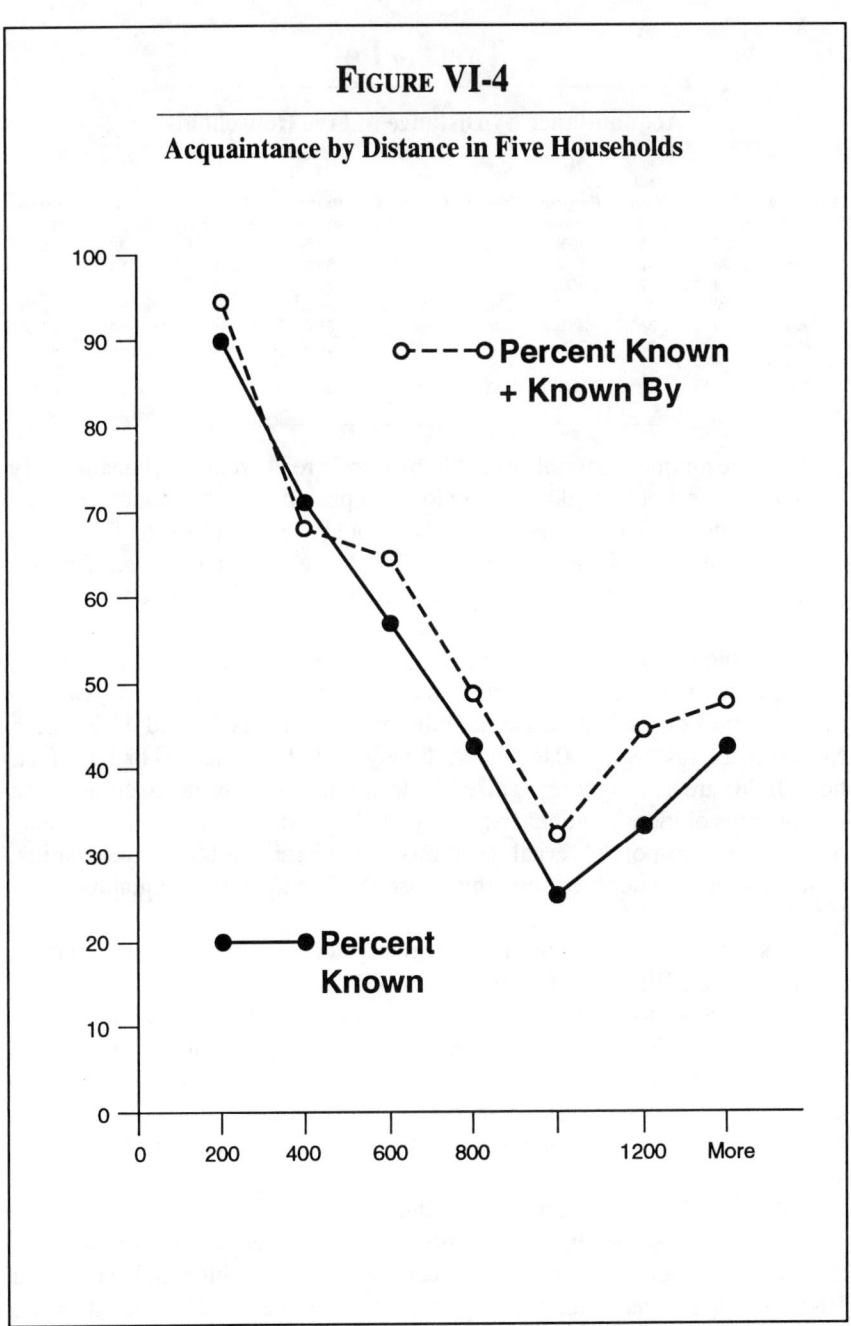

FIGURE VI-4

Acquaintance by Distance in Five Households

TABLE VI-4

Acquaintance by Distance in Five Households

Distance in Feet	Known	Could Have Known	Percent Known	Known By	Could Be Known By	Percent Known By	Known + Known By	K + K Possible	Percent K + K
200	25	28	89%	11	11	100%	36	39	92%
400	32	42	71%	6	11	55%	38	56	68%
600	29	52	56%	17	22	77%	46	74	62%
800	19	45	42%	10	17	59%	29	62	47%
1000	10	38	26%	6	11	55%	16	49	32%
1200	11	32	34%	7	12	58%	18	44	41%
More than 1200	22	52	42	13	21	62%	35	73	48%

With the numbers possible to be "known by" greatly reduced, because only surveyed households could be included, the percentages did not seem to be closely related to distance. But when "known bys" were added to "knowns," the pattern of knowns was not changed. There was a decline in identification until 1000 feet, then an increase thereafter. The parallel declines are shown in Figure VI-4.

So without neighborhoods being considered, there was a decline in recognition for a distance greater than the length of any neighborhood. The two most distant houses in a single neighborhood, numbers 33 and 43 in south Millfield, are just over 800 feet apart. It may be that beyond 800 or 1000 feet, households are no longer recognized by location alone, instead needing some other means of identification: friendship, daily passing on the way to the post office, street-to-porch verbal relationships, shared hobby relationships, acquaintance at school, or something else that would relate acquaintance to location.

This suggests that there might be greater acquaintance in adjacent neighborhoods. With only four neighborhoods, however, there is not much to check. All neighborhoods are adjacent to central Millfield, while Hickory Street and south Millfield are adjacent to each other. Only north Millfield is separated by central Millfield from Hickory Street and south Millfield. This does suggest, however, one reason why north Millfield residents might have been less acquainted with other neighborhoods than were residents in the other areas.

Table VI-5 shows that adjacency did make a difference. In every case, families were able to identify more households in an adjacent neighborhood than in a neighborhood separated by central Millfield. This reinforces Table VI-3, which showed that in every case families were able to identify the

TABLE VI-5

Acquaintances in Adjacent and Separated Neighborhoods

	Adjacent			Separated		
	Knew	Could Know	Percentage	Knew	Could Know	Percent
North Millfield	22	105	21%	24	203	12%
Central Millfield	78	230	34%	0	0	00%
South Millfield	65	165	39%	27	85	32%
Hickory Street	65	130	50%	34	85	40%
Total	230	630	37%	85	373	23%

occupants of more houses in their own neighborhood than in Millfield as a whole. Propinquity matters.

So, measured by knowledge of where people live, there is evidence for neighborhoods in a community as small as Millfield. People are more likely to know who lives where in their own neighborhood and more likely to know where people live in the next neighborhood than in the one beyond. And in this sense, the names for the neighborhoods have some validity beyond geographical justification.

On the other hand, it could be argued that neighborhoods are, to some extent, a function of distance, at least up to 1000 feet, or a five minute walk. People are more likely to know where other people live because they are nearby, not because they are in the same or an adjacent neighborhood.

There is one other geographical reason for knowing where people live, and this is related to intimacy creating functions that are believed to be performed by local centers such as the grocery store, the soda fountain, or, in the case of Millfield, the post office. The image in Millfield is that people walk to the post office to pick up their mail (except for one or two houses in north Millfield that are on a mail delivery route). The image is certainly confirmed on a Saturday, where people are indeed seen to be chatting outside the post office. The image also says that people going to and from the post office may chat with people

TABLE VI-6

The Influence of the Post Office

	Route of the Post Office	Opposite Direction
Households Identified	118	78
Possible Identifications	160	161
Percent Identified	74%	48%

sitting on porches or working in their front yards. If that is the case, it is possible that people may recognize one another at the post office, but not be exactly sure where an acquaintance lives. And those who chat with yard workers would know where the yard workers live, but the yard workers might not know exactly where the strollers live, except further down the street from the post office. If that were so, we should expect that families would be able to identify a higher percentage of households on the route to the post office than in the opposite direction. So, for instance, the family living at 59 Hickory Street would be more likely to be able to identify houses along Hickory Street toward the post office than away.

The ever-accommodating Table VI-1 grid provides the necessary information to answer this question. We checked each of the twenty-two families who answered the map questions except one north Millfield family that was on a mail delivery route. In each case we compared the identified households located toward the post office with those on the same street in the opposite direction. Our results are summarized in the very brief Table VI-6, which confirms the image. At least the results are what one would expect if the post office has the influence Millfielders think it has and social theorists say it would have.

Networks Disregarding Area

We have seen that most of the perceived geographical identifications have some validity in relation to acquaintances. People really do seem to know more people who live in the same neighborhood, more who live in adjacent rather than separated neighborhoods, more who live closer than farther away, and more who live on the route to the post office than in the other direction. We have, however, in our theory chapter, endorsed the idea that the acquaintance is more important than the area. So let us see if neighborhoods can be defined in terms of networks of acquaintances.

It would seem that all we would need to do is take a map and draw arrows from the sample households to all the households of the community, and then we should be able to see at a glance what the "real" neighborhoods are. Well, perhaps somewhere someone has a computer that will do this, but we are not so fortunate. When we first attempted to draw the arrows, we soon had an incomprehensible mess. Then we tried schematizing the map, as if the houses were located around a squarish oval. That was still a mess. We thought we would draw a schematized map, to show what happens, and we were just going to show the relationships of south Millfield. But by the time we had drawn such relationships for only three houses, the diagram was already becoming incomprehensible. Figure VI-5 shows the interim result with lines drawn only from houses 35, 38, and 40 of south Millfield. The double lines are neighborhood boundaries. There may be some other way in which this can be done. We haven't found it. And if the representation is so complicated that it cannot be grasped, is it of any value?

It is, of course, possible to draw the network for an individual household. Perhaps the neighborhood could be drawn as an area if the households identified were circled. This might be more representative, too, in that the householder doesn't have direct connections, only recognition that as he passes a house he knows someone who lives there. Circling also has the advantage of clarity. The disadvantage may be that it does not reflect network as well as lines between houses.

We looked for a household with something near the median number of identifications (twenty-two) and tried household number 25 in central Millfield. The eighteen identifications are shown by the numbered households in Figure VI-6, with the extremes left out. The justification for this is that if householders from house 25 walk north of the church, they would not know who lives in any of the houses on Millfield Road. If they walked beyond house 51 in the Hickory Street area, they would know only the last house. This suggests that these houses are known for other reasons. So the neighborhood, for the householders of house 25, might be identified by the area circled.

Now, let's take a household with few identifications. We randomly chose the third fewest (which turned out to be a tie) and used house 12 in north Millfield. This time the neighborhood, a small one, is easily identified (Figure VI-7). It covers less than north Millfield and doesn't stray outside. Let's

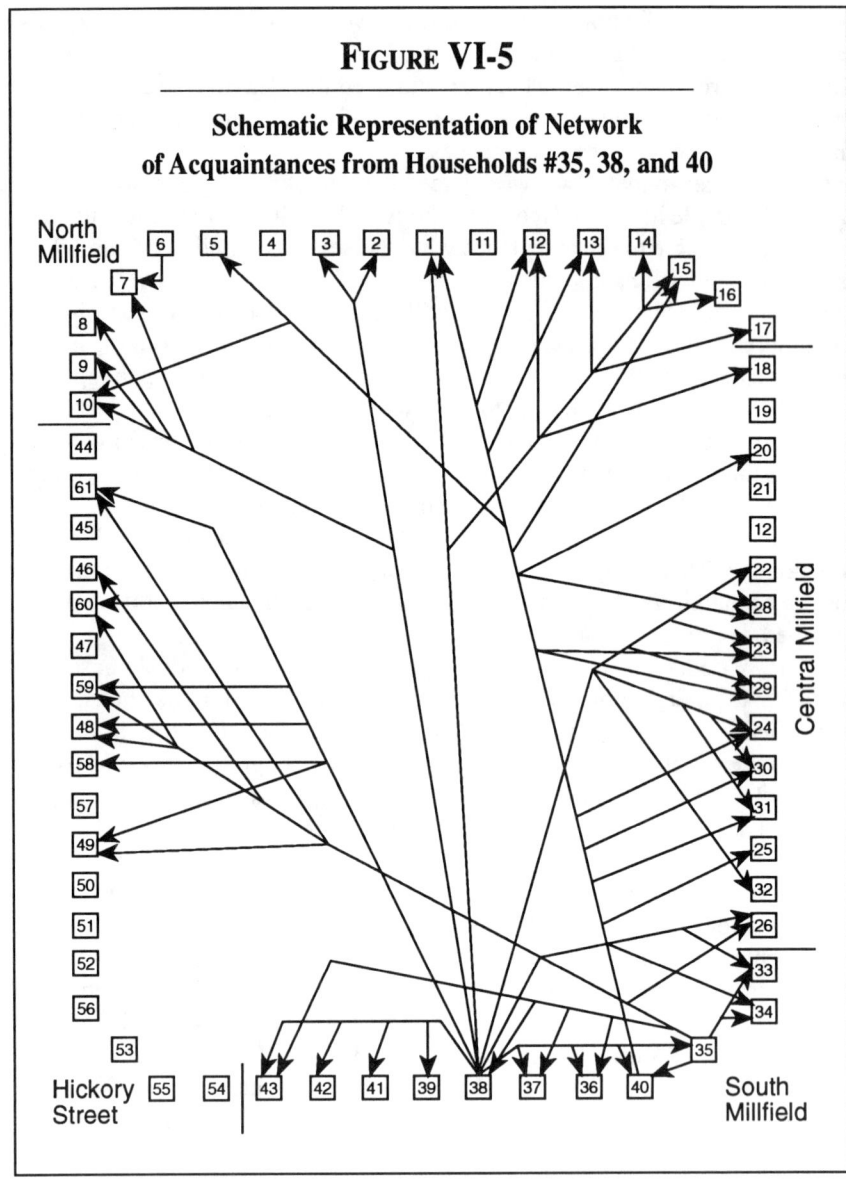

FIGURE VI-5

Schematic Representation of Network
of Acquaintances from Households #35, 38, and 40

Figure VI-6

Neighborhood of Household 25

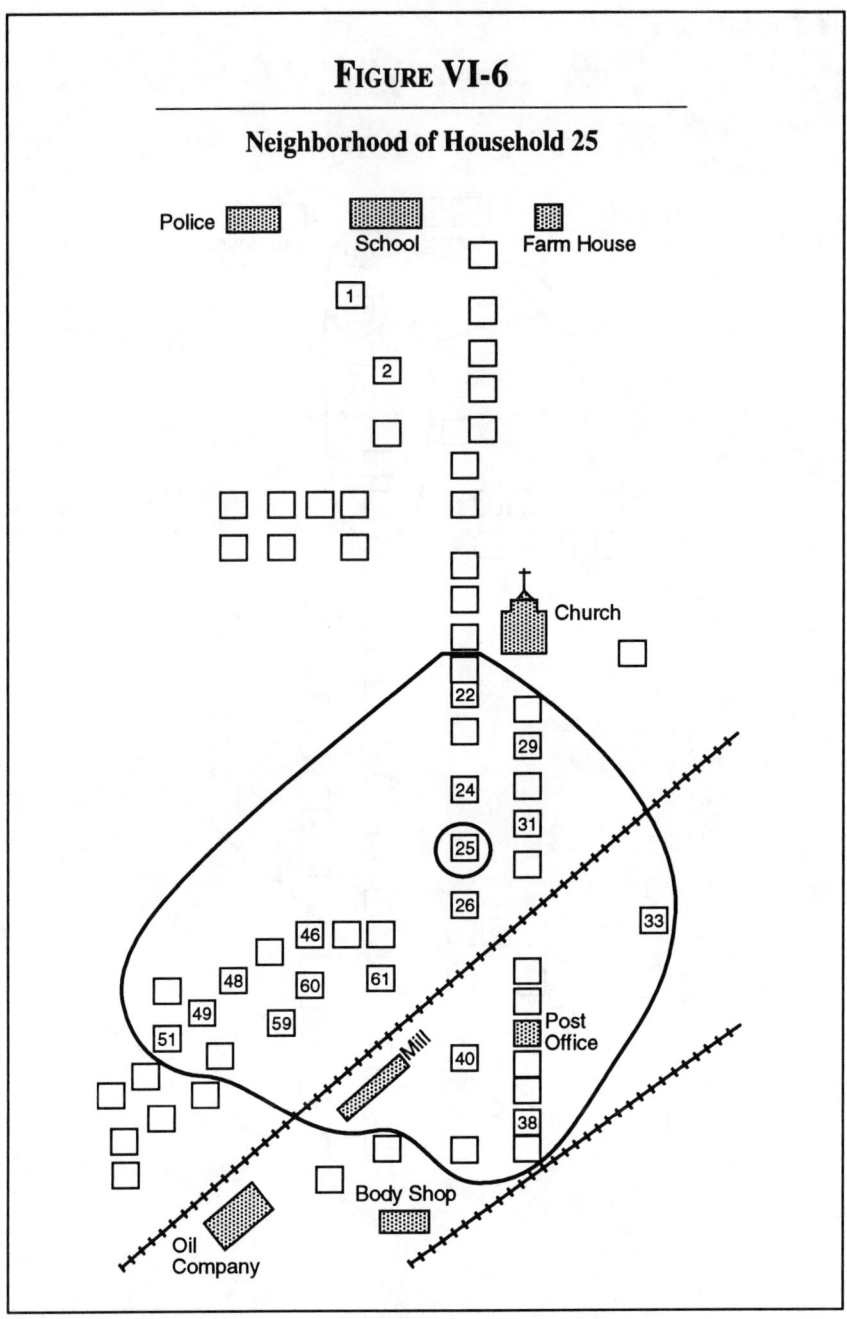

92 Millfield on Saturday: Searching for Community in a Metropolitan Village

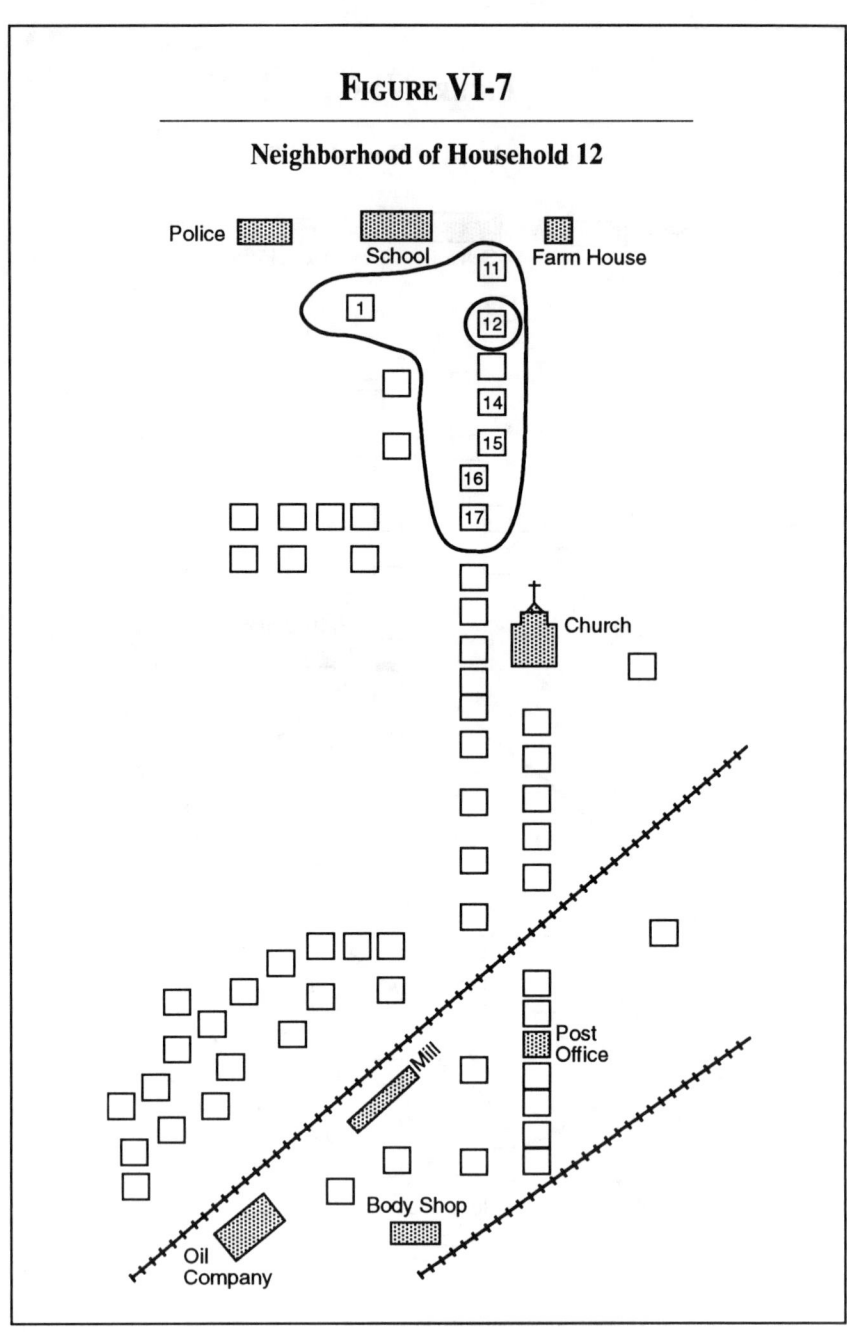

FIGURE VI-7

Neighborhood of Household 12

Circles of Aquaintance 93

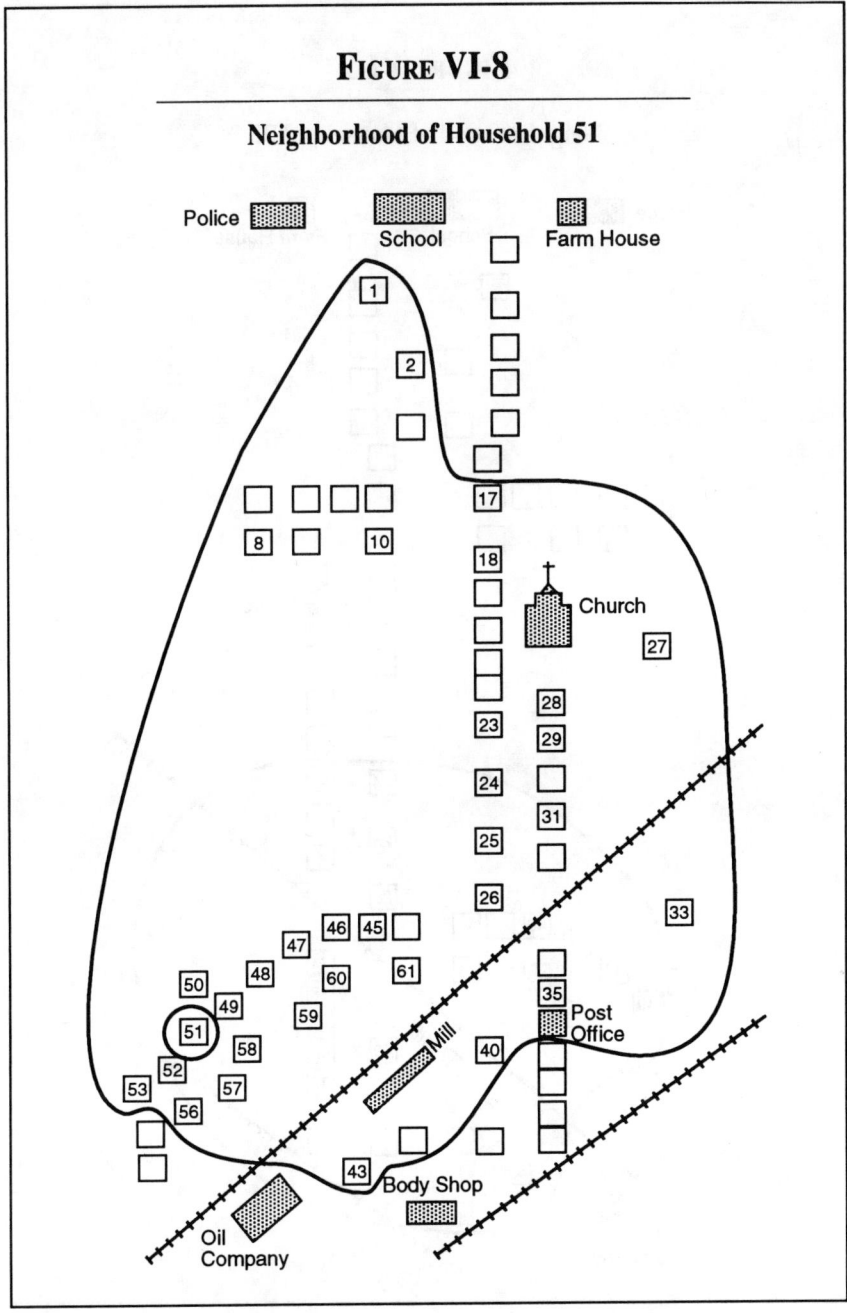

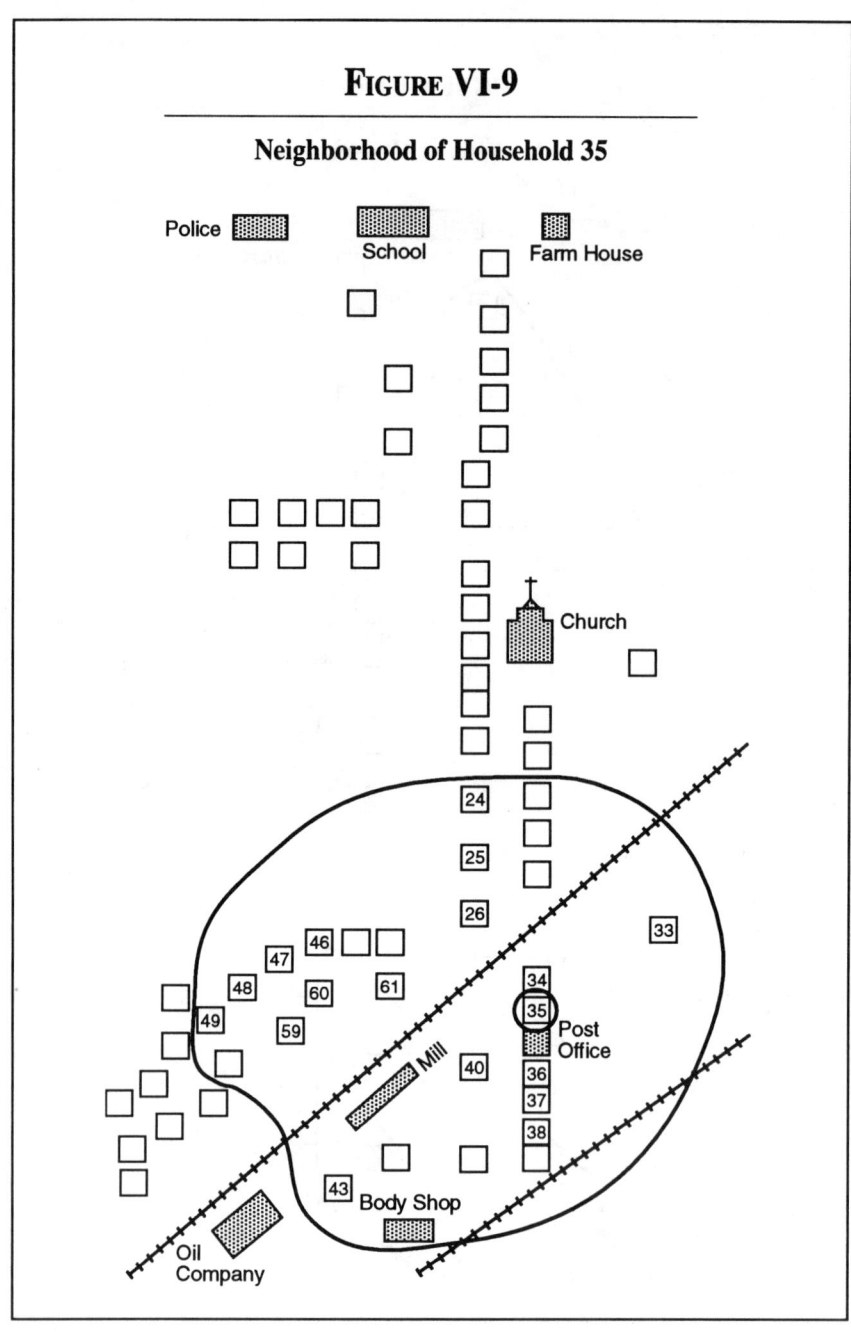

FIGURE VI-9

Neighborhood of Household 35

FIGURE VI-10

South Millfield's Neighborhood

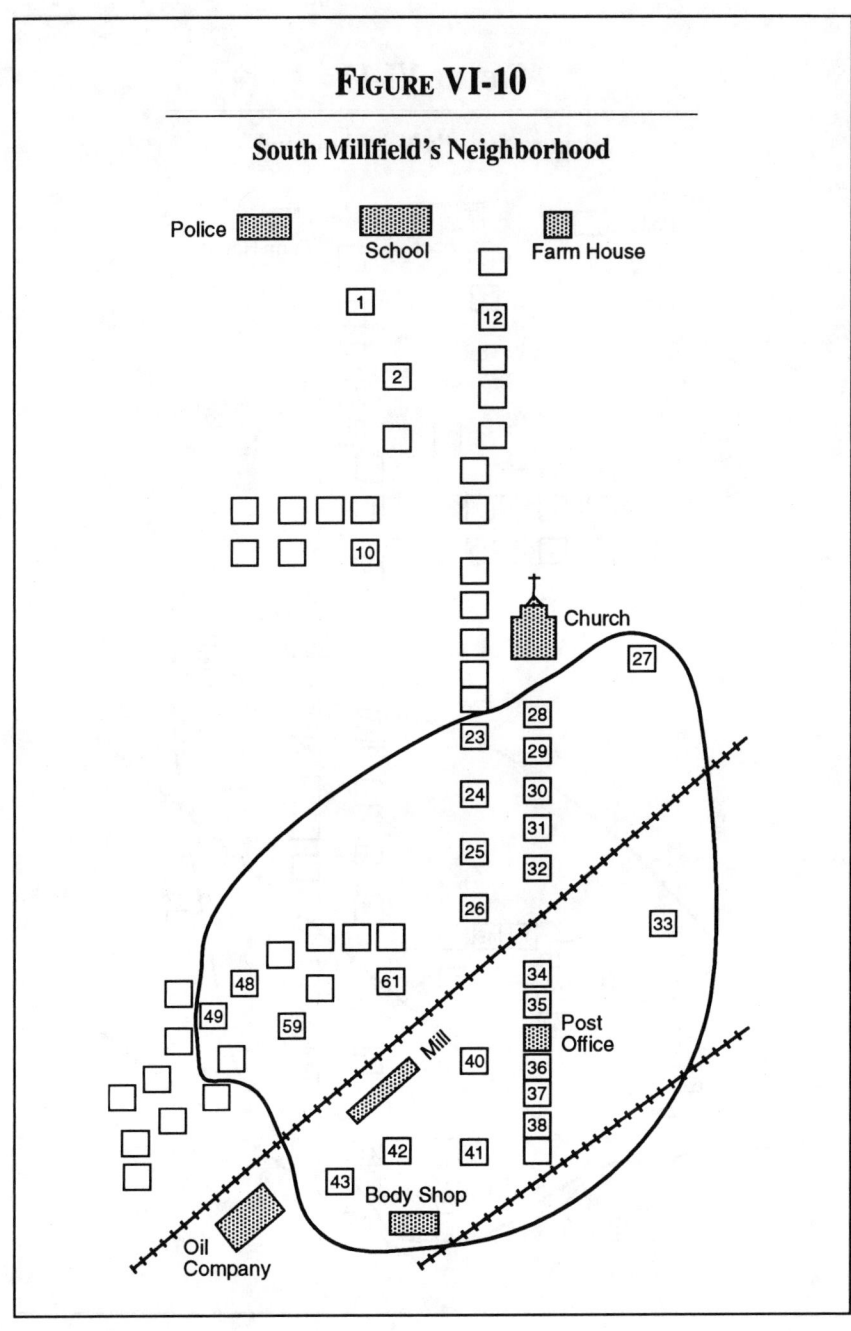

96 Millfield on Saturday: Searching for Community in a Metropolitan Village

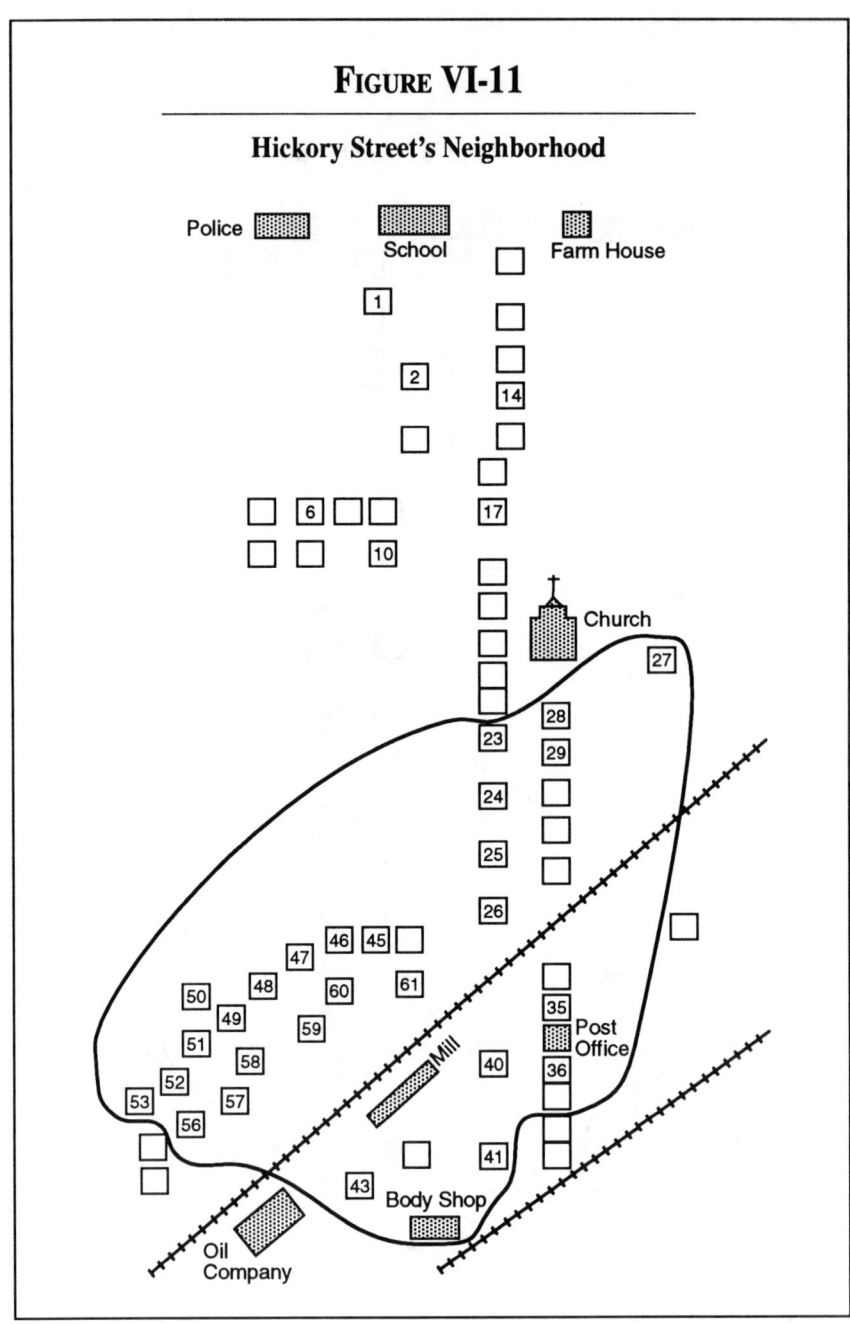

FIGURE VI-11

Hickory Street's Neighborhood

Circles of Aquaintance 97

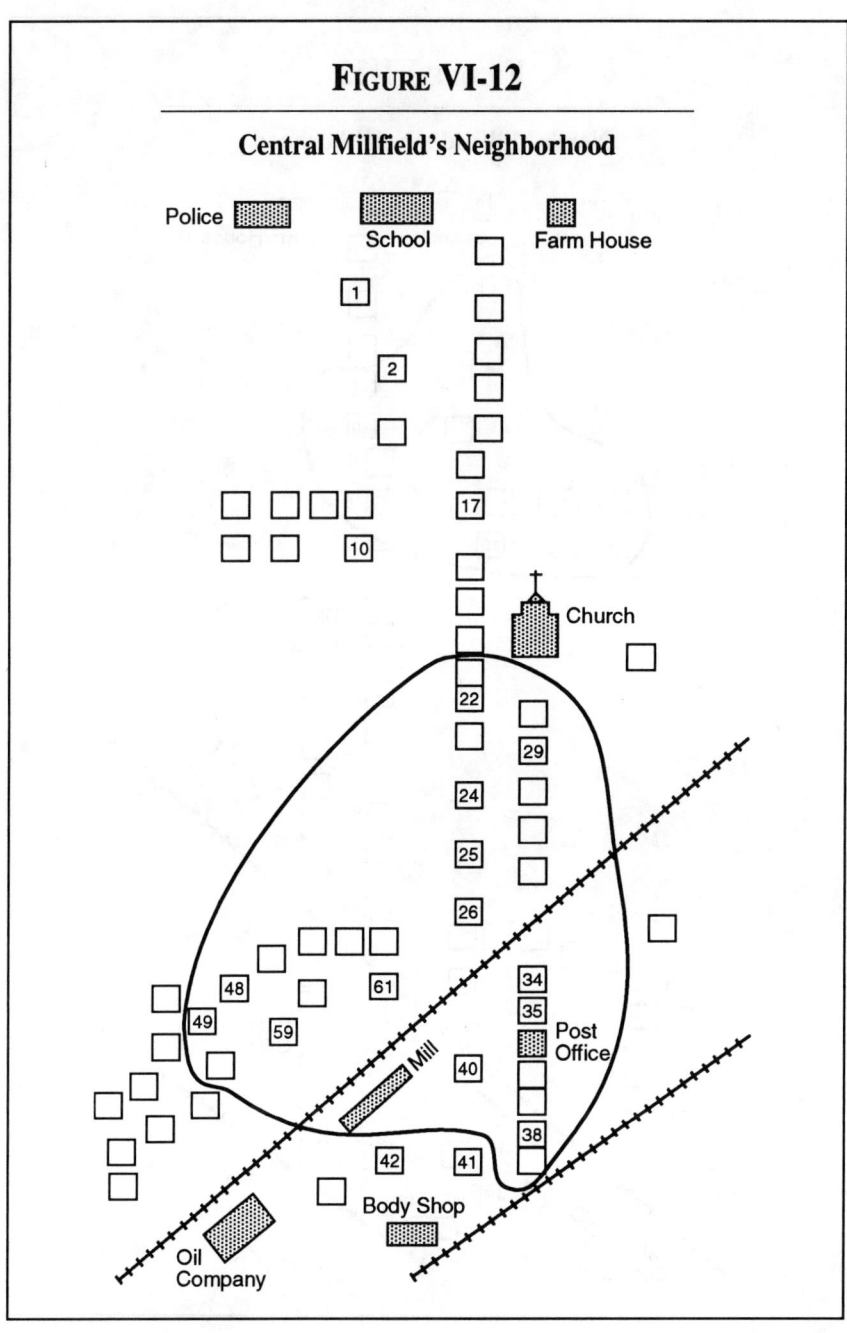

FIGURE VI-12

Central Millfield's Neighborhood

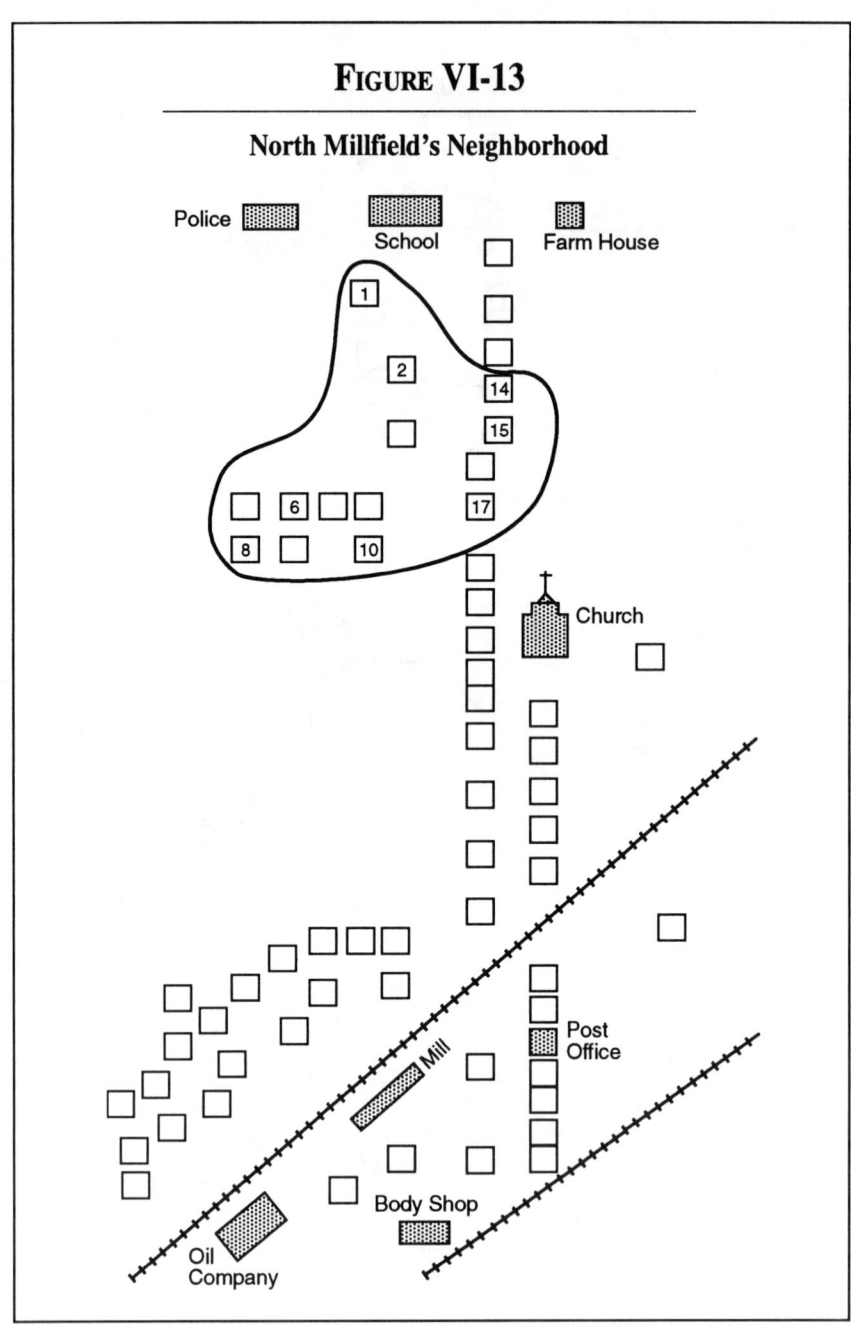

FIGURE VI-13

North Millfield's Neighborhood

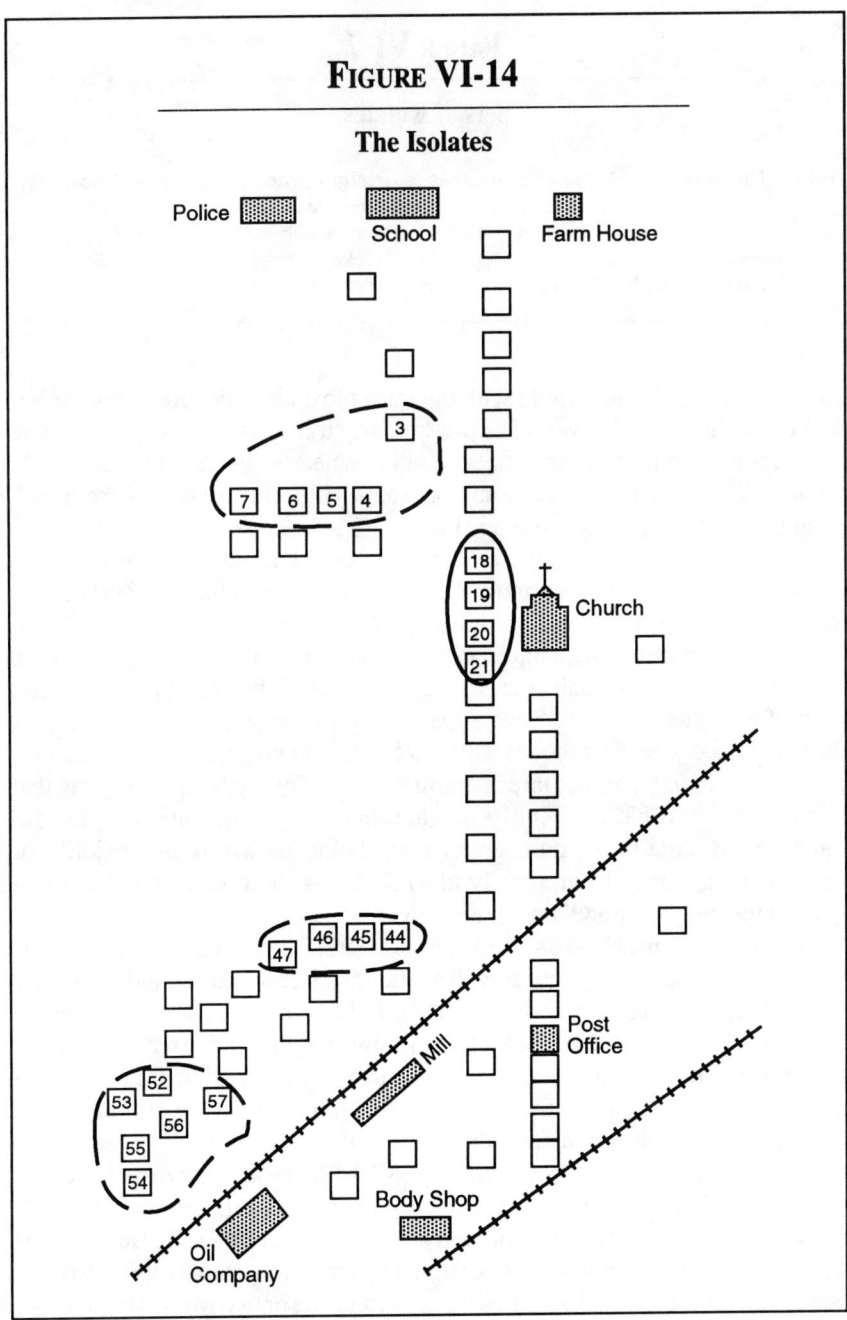

TABLE VI-7

Sets of Isolates

House Numbers	Number of Houses	Neighborhood	Mean Known By
3–7	5	North Millfield	4.8
18–21	4	Central Millfield	5.75
44–47	4	Hickory Street	5
52–57	6	Hickory Street	4.5

compare that to the household with the third most identifications (Figure VI-8). For this household, it would be pretty nearly true to say that Millfield is one big neighborhood. The range of acquaintances nearly encompasses the whole village. We also took one at random from south Millfield, to have one from each neighborhood. This was house 35 (Figure VI-9).

We presume, in setting these neighborhoods, that you wouldn't have to know the occupants of every household for comfort, but if they are fairly close, this would solidify neighborhood identity. Drawn this way, in these four cases, the household with few acquaintances encompassed less than one neighborhood. The one with most acquaintances encompassed two full neighborhoods and parts of two others. House 35 encompassed its own neighborhood and parts of the two adjacent neighborhoods. House 25, while having more acquaintances, encompassed only parts of three neighborhoods. This approach suggests that it might be possible to identify neighborhoods by acquaintance after all. Suppose we write in the numbers of households known by the majority of households in each of our already identified neighborhoods? Wouldn't that give us the neighborhood's neighborhood?

The maps (Figures VI-10–VI-13) show rather similar looking neighborhoods for central and south Millfield as well as Hickory Street, each including houses in the other two neighborhoods. North Millfield, by contrast, appears isolated, with identifications taking place only in its own neighborhood. By this kind of measure, it might be argued that there are only two neighborhoods in Millfield, a larger one to the south, a smaller one to the north, with three or four houses opposite the church serving as a divider.

These four houses are shown in Figure VI-14. They are known by relatively few people (4, 7, 6, and 6). The church does not act as a unifier in that people come to it from outside the community, mostly on Sundays. It also occupies territory that otherwise would be occupied by other houses that might not have been isolates. If there had been houses there, and one or two were at the average

Table VI-8

Households in Neighborhoods' "Neighborhoods"

Neighborhood	Households Known by Majority	Houses Known in "Neighborhood"	Houses in "Neighborhood"
North Millfield	8	8	14
Central Millfield	16	12	28
South Millfield	28	24	31
Hickory Street	33	27	36
Consolidation Millfield South	25	21	35

level known (10), north Millfielders might have known more people to the south, and residents of other areas might have known more to the north. The distance created by the isolates is about 300 feet.

The term "isolates" is not intended to be pejorative. These four households were known by relatively few in the sample, but there were other groups of houses with low visibility (Table VI-7). The group from 3 to 7 in north Millfield and 44 to 47 on Hickory Street did not break the web of familiarity because there were houses on the other side of the street occupied by families that were better known (Figure VI-14). This couldn't happen in the central Millfield set because the church happened to be across the street. Houses 52–57 on Hickory Street occupied opposite sides of the street, but they are at the end of the block and therefore can perform no separating function. It is surprising to find two such isolated sets on Hickory Street, where the sample had the greatest familiarity with both neighborhood and Millfield as a whole.

Table VI-8 shows the houses known by the majority in the sample of each neighborhood. The number of these that would seem to belong to the neighborhood's "neighborhood," and the total number of houses in the "neighborhoods" thus designated. The overlapping of the three neighborhoods south of the church suggests that, by using the same method, we could find a single neighborhood drawn around houses known by the majority in the sample from those neighborhoods. There were fifteen houses in those neighborhoods and Figure VI-15 shows the neighborhood (consolidated Millfield south). As Table VI-8 shows, it is actually smaller than the Hickory Street neighborhood of Figure VI-11.

It could be argued that the four neighborhoods are valid if you perceive either geographical area or general perception, and that this validity is reinforced by greater knowledge of households in one's own neighborhood so designated and greater knowledge of households in an adjacent neighborhood

102 Millfield on Saturday: Searching for Community in a Metropolitan Village

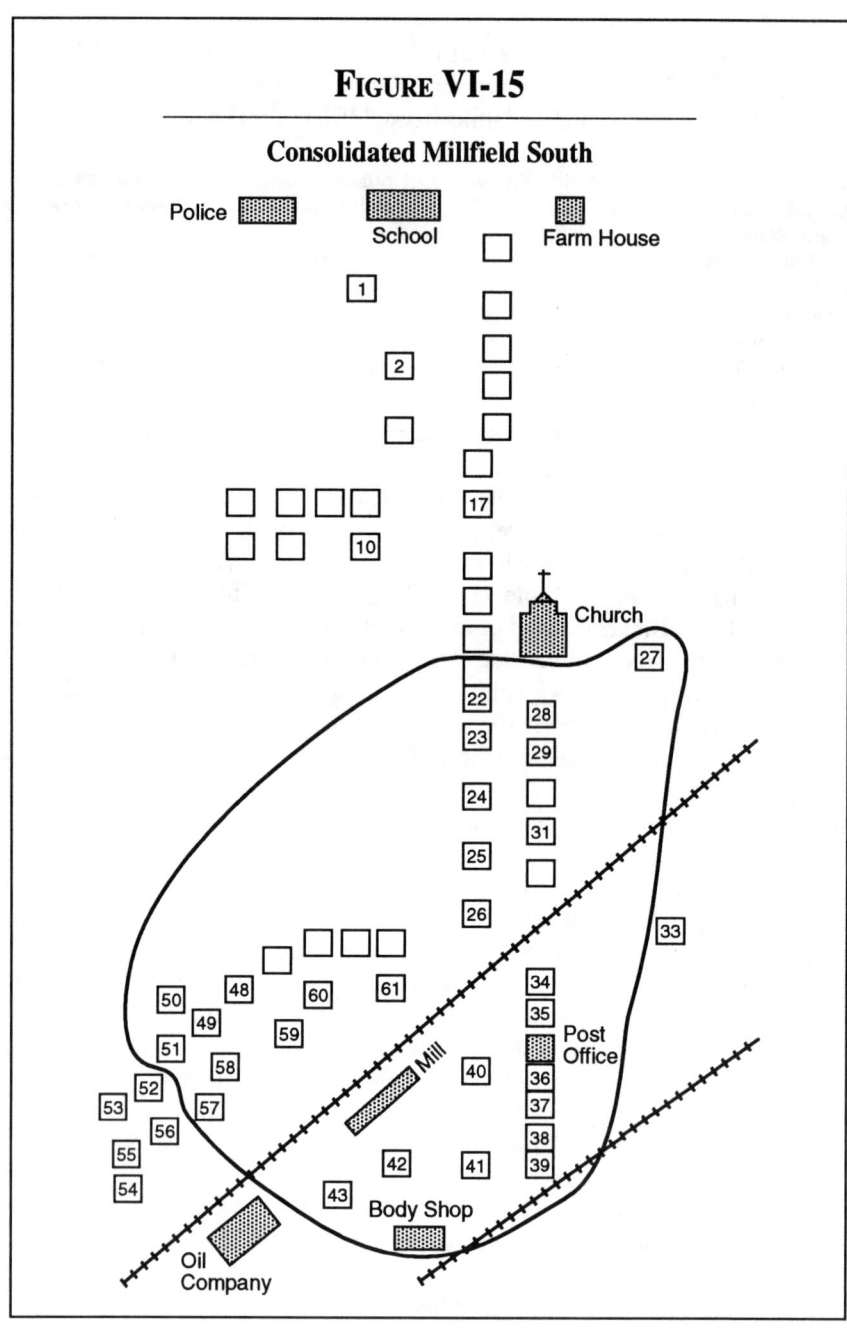

compared to a separated neighborhood.

On the other hand it could be argued that Millfield has only two neighborhoods—north Millfield and Millfield south—if you base your judgment on households known by a majority of householders in a contiguous area. This approach gives greater weight to households known, with contiguous area defined by that knowledge rather than landmarks, area names, or general perception.

Possibly the difficulty in attempting to determine neighborhoods by acquaintance is the use of the term "networks." Perhaps the image given by the concept of net is one of lines drawn between points, which brings about the confusion suggested in Figure VI-5. Not only is this confusing, but it isn't as representative as a circle, because in a neighborhood people don't go from house to house; they are simply aware of the occupants of some, but not all, of the other houses in the neighborhood. So we can with some justification use the metaphors "lines of friendship" and "circles of acquaintance."

Education and Length of Residence

The ways of testing relationships in five dozen households seem to be almost infinite. Every time one tests something, it seems that two more possible tests are suggested. But many of the theoretical concerns have now been addressed. Three more seem worth pursuing at this point: education, length of residence, and friendship.

Length of residence is mentioned frequently in community theory. It is supposed to be one of the strongest measures of neighborhood and community acquaintance. If you live a long time in a neighborhood, you'll know more people in the surrounding area and be known by more people.

Education is less frequently mentioned, perhaps because it is assumed that people living in the same neighborhood will have similar education and status. We have seen, however, that people living on Hickory Street had a better knowledge of the total community than those living in any of the other neighborhoods. And occasionally perhaps, there was the slightest whiff of condescension for Hickory Street. It wasn't what it had been, and one may tolerate its insularity as a testimony to the community spirit of Millfield.

We had asked about years of education and had distinguished textbook from colloquial grammar, so we had two measures of education. Could it be that people with more years of education are better known and perhaps people with fewer years of education know more people? We can test that and see if it has any application to Hickory Street.

Finally, we have the question of best friends. Silverman (1987) had

TABLE VI-9

Acquaintance and Length of Residence

Years in Millfield	Number	Mean Known	Percent of Households	Mean Known By	Percent of Sample
0–5	6	13	21	6	27
0–10	9	17	28	8	36
10–20	5	27	44	11	50
20–40	3	27	44	12	55
50–70	5	21	34	13	59

suggested that friends and neighbors should be considered separately and that neighbors are not likely to be considered friends. We have already considerable support for that, having seen in the previous chapter that Millfielders interact more with kin and friends outside of Millfield than they do with those inside. We have also seen that fewer than 10 percent of the acquaintances within Millfield were considered friends.

Let's take up length of residence first, because that's easiest, then education. Finally, we'll look at the data, thus far neglected, on friends who live in the community.

Table VI-9 shows an attempt to relate acquaintance to length of residence. The results are clear enough, but the numbers are too small for significance. The table shows the relation between length of residence and the number of households identified as well as the number who were able to identify a member of each sample household. The length of residence was that of the household member who had lived in Millfield longest. The number of households listed is greater than the number sampled, because those who had lived in Millfield for five years or less were used in both the 0–5 and 0–10 categories.

In Millfield the number of people known increased with residence for the first twenty years, peaked at that point, and declined for those who had lived in Millfield more than fifty years. The number of people one was "known by" increased with residence throughout, but only slowly after twenty years. Residents who lived in Millfield for five years knew about half the number of residents that were known by those living there between ten and forty years. The same is true among those known by others. It would appear new residents soon were acquainted with a substantial percentage of households in the village, then gradually got to know as many more over a much longer period. Of course, people were also moving in and out during this time. It may be that

Table VI-10

Acquaintance and Education

	Mean Known	Mean Known By
Textbook Grammar	21	9
College Education	21	11
Colloquial Grammar	21	11
High School Education	20	9

older people are less mobile, and begin to lose familiarity as new people move in. On the other hand, because of their longevity, they remain as well known as they were in their more active days. Millfield, in this respect, seems similar to other communities.

Expectations that education might affect status and the number of people by whom one was known were not confirmed. Table VI-10 indicates that education and grammar did not seem to be important factors either in knowing people or being known. There was very little difference in households who spoke textbook grammar as opposed to those who spoke colloquial grammar and very little between those who had a college education and those who had not been to college.

Friends in the Community

Tables VI-1 and VI-2 distinguish friends from acquaintances, but thus far, we have treated them as similar. After members of a household had looked at a map, they were asked if anyone in any of the households identified had been considered one of their three best friends. The question made it possible for no best friend to be identified, if one's best friend lived outside. Best friends living in the same house, of course, were also excluded. It would also be possible for more than three best friends to be identified, since we were interviewing families.

The first thing that is obvious from Table VI-1 is that there are many more Ks than Fs. As Silverman suggests, neighbors are mostly acquaintances, perhaps of the nodding sort. Only 6 percent of the households identified contained friends, only 6 percent of the sample were identified as friends by others.

This time, because there are relatively few and because lines of friendship seem appropriate, as distinguished from circle of acquaintances, the lines can

106   Millfield on Saturday: Searching for Community in a Metropolitan Village

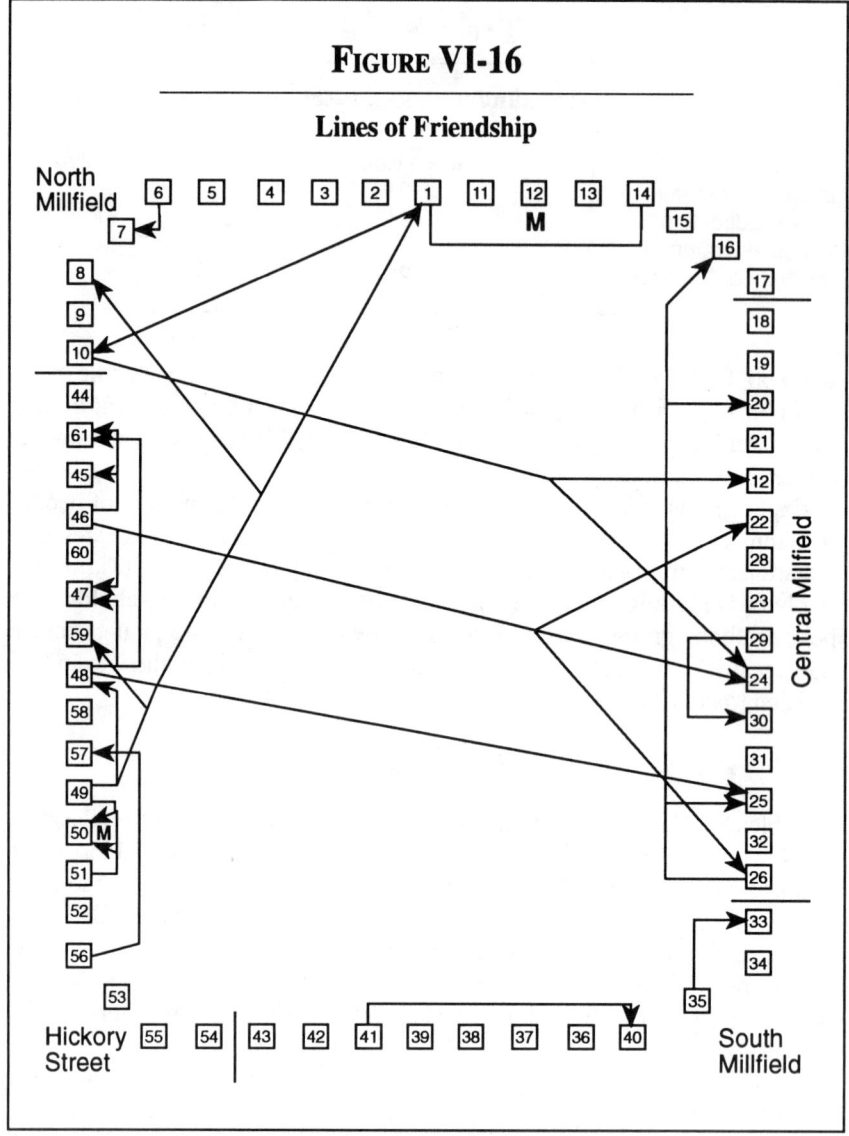

TABLE VI-11

Friends by Neighborhoods

Neighborhood	Total Friends	Total Identified as Friends	Sample Identified as Friends	Mutual Friends	Friends Outside Neighborhood	Identified Outside Neighborhood
North Millfield	6	7	5	1	2	3
Central Millfield	4	9	5	0	1	6
South Millfield	2	2	1	0	0	0
Hickory	18	12	3	1	6	0

be drawn directly from house to house (Figure VI-16). A table (VI-11) of friendships can be made by combining information from Table VI-1 and Figure VI-16.

Figure VI-16 shows the lines of friendship running from the household that identified the friend to the friend's house. An immediate look at the figure suggests great interaction on Hickory Street and quite a bit in central Millfield. Next, there seemed to be a great many arrows circulating within Hickory Street, but quite a few shooting across the diagram, mostly from Hickory Street to central Millfield, actually an adjacent neighborhood.

We had some feeling that Hickory Street might have been a socially slightly inferior neighborhood, but that is weak anecdotal evidence not borne out by the educational and colloquial measures. We have established that Hickory Street was the neighborhood with the highest level of acquaintance both within and without the neighborhood (Table VI-3). This appears to carryover into friendships, with eighteen friends identified by the sample from Hickory Street.

It is true that Hickory Streeters are more likely to identify friends outside the neighborhood, most of them in adjacent central Millfield. Central Millfielders, less gregarious, are more frequently identified as friends than they are likely to identify friends outside the neighborhood. The hunch that people might be upwardly mobile in their identification of friends was not supported. Because one household had two adults with different educational levels and grammar and another was involved in five of the fourteen situations in which someone in the sample was identified as a friend, there were only nine remaining cases. In five of these there were friendships between high school colloquials and two were between college textbooks. In the other two cases a colloquial identified a textbook, as our hypothesis had expected, and a textbook identified a colloquial.

At first glance, the fact that there were only two mutual friends in the sample seemed shocking. Almost everyone who identified a best friend was not so identified in return. Usually, when someone says, "the lady across the street is my best friend," you assume reciprocity. But on reflection, we recalled that our question requested three best friends. The person not identified might have been considered a good friend, but not among the three best in the whole world.

Generally, the findings support Silverman's view that neighborhoods provide support rather than friendship. Out of the neighborhood you may happen to have one or two friends, but providing friendship does not seem to be a major function of the neighborhoods or of Millfield as a community.

Recapitulation

"Everyone knows everyone" does not mean that everyone knows where everyone lives. Households in the sample were able to identify a particular house in which another villager lived in only 37 percent of possible identifications. In each area-defined neighborhood, householders identified residents in a higher percentage of other households in their own neighborhood than they could in any other. They also made a higher percentage of identifications in adjacent neighborhoods than they could in separated neighborhoods. Could this have been a function of distance rather than neighborhoods? Up to 1000 feet it could, for at 200-foot intervals there was positive correlation between propinquity and ability to identify. Beyond 1000 feet the correlation no longer held.

The image of a local center being a factor in acquaintance was supported by the Millfield data. People did indeed know better where others lived on the route to the post office than they did in the opposite direction.

When neighborhoods were drawn by circles of acquaintance rather than by recognized landmarks, a somewhat different configuration emerged. The three southern neighborhoods overlapped considerably. Only north Millfield remained separated. By this approach Millfield could be described as having two neighborhoods: north Millfield and consolidated Millfield south. One possible explanation for the separation would be the combination of four houses with a fewer than average number of acquaintances across the street from the church, the combination acting as a 300-foot semiporous separator.

Length of residence correlated with households known up to twenty years, stabilized from that time until fifty years when it began to decline. On the other hand, the longer you lived in Millfield, the more likely you were to be known by others. No correlations were established between measures of education and circles of acquaintance. And as for friends, only 6 percent of the acquaintances in the community were identified as best friends. The neighborhood appears to supply general support rather than specific friendships.

Chapter VII

Memories of the Past, Fears for the Future: When the City Is at the Gates

Like many urban areas, greater Brixton has expanded in the past thirty years. The expanding population of the postwar baby boom, the building of two interstate highways, and governmental encouragement of building new housing rather than renovating the old has led to a great increase in the suburban population, the building of thousands of brick, ranch-style houses, and the concomitant development of numerous shopping centers in what had been outlying areas.

One of the consequences of this expansion is that autonomous farming villages near Brixton have been surrounded by the suburbs, and the farmland has been sold. Sometimes the village remains the center of town. The oldest and often most charming houses are at the heart of the business district. At other times, as in the case of Millfield, the suburban center is elsewhere and the village becomes a distinctive but nevertheless incidental part of the sprawling suburb.

The suburb surrounding Millfield is Coopertown. On a 1955 map, Coopertown is a rural township, Millfield a separate village. By 1985 the population of Coopertown had reached thirty thousand, and it was characterized by brick ranch houses on large lots and a scattered business district. Millfield still appears to be a separate village of sixty houses, most of them clapboard, the majority two story. The houses are closer together, the lots are smaller. The majority have front porches, and there's an absence of sidewalks. It still looks like the country village it was thirty years ago.

But we know it isn't. The members of the sixty households no longer make their living from farming. Most of the residents drive to work along Route 69 to Brixton, in the opposite direction to the nearby satellite city of Corinth, or to Coopertown itself (Figure I-1). There are only three visible businesses in the town: Engelbrecht's Body Shop, Dewsberry Oil Company, and Millfield Seed and Grain. Millfield Seed and Grain, a striking landmark, is no longer functioning.

Millfield, then, is not the farm village it appears to be. Surely it has experienced a great deal of change in the past three decades, as Brixton and Cooperfield expanded. To what extent can it have remained a quiet village community with the city at the gates? Has a vast internal social change taken place? Are the residents aware of the change? Do they fear further change in the future?

Hypotheses

What seemed likely? To begin with, we know that many people who live in Millfield are aware of the apparent peaceful community atmosphere. And they want to maintain it. Therefore, they would be more likely to perceive changes in the past than to want change in the future. They would want Millfield to remain as it is. On the other hand, people would be apprehensive about the changes they have experienced, and we wouldn't be surprised if long-time residents had a sense of the good old days, a feeling that things were better in the past than they are now.

It seemed likely that other urban people would react as the visiting sociologists did. What a neat place to live! Therefore, some of the houses may have been bought by people working in greater Brixton who were attracted by this vestige of apparent community in a sea of opulent but anonymous ranch houses. On the other hand, there would be other residents who had lived there longer, who bought when housing was cheaper, or who inherited their houses. Would there be any conflict between newcomers and established residents about how Millfield is or should be? We thought there might. There probably would be some agreement that Millfield should be maintained. But wouldn't the people moving in, with better educations and urban backgrounds, want to keep the village as it is, but beautifully restored? The rural people, on the other hand, while they would want it keep as it is, would not be concerned about restoration and would want freedom to continue doing whatever they like to do, regardless of how that might affect the appearance of the village.

Further the rural, less-educated dwellers might be more willing to accept urban improvements such as streetlights, sidewalks, and home-delivered mail. The urbanites would be more willing to forego these improvements or even resist them in order to keep the village a village.

We thought there might be a difference in perceptions of history. The urban-educated would be likely to have a more complete set of information about Millfield than the rural people who had lived there a short time. Long-time residents, on the other hand, would have more information about past activities, without concern about their historical significance. We thought all residents would be more likely to perceive change in symbols and things than in people, because these were more visible when considering change and because of a shared desire that the village really not change.

We also expected that the expansion of Brixton and the incorporation of Millfield into Coopertown must have more of an effect than is visible. We expected that all residents were likely to fear building and development near Millfield, with a resultant disappearance of cornfields, increase in traffic, and other changes that would undermine village tranquility.

But we did not expect these apprehensions really to be deep. We thought that people might expect to leave Millfield, if at all, because a change in jobs forced them to move elsewhere or because their children grew up and their house was too big to maintain. We did not expect that they would really be worried about being forced to move by some external catastrophic change, such as the bulldozing of Millfield to make another shopping mall.

Past Change, Coming Change

It turned out that despite the city appearing to be rather dramatically "at the gates," the prevailing perception was that Millfield had changed little and was not likely to change. In fifteen of the twenty-four households there was a distinct perception that little had changed, even from people who knew quite a bit about the history of Millfield or from old-timers who could remember quite a number of specific changes. People were a little more wary of predicting the future, but in ten households the expectation was that there would be little change. Only members of three households mentioned change in the past, and only one of these clearly thought the change was important. In only two households was important change anticipated in the future.

Many of the comments on change in the past were laconic. "No big changes goin' on." "Hasn't changed much." "Can't see any change." "Really hasn't changed." And the firmest statement: "Hasn't changed a lick. It's still the same as when I moved here." Others noted that there had been change but it wasn't anything important. "Not in any important way I can think of." The post office changed from one building to another, but both buildings were small. "We've had the same mailbox ever since we've come, Box 36." One group of residents "lived here for umpteen years," but now they are "starting to pass away and what have you; but then the residents that are living here now look like they're gonna be here for umpteen years. I mean there's not a big turnover."

One vivid summary of this viewpoint: "The quaintness of the area is that if you could actually roll back in time—the color of the houses may have changed, but they're the same houses. Nobody's added on a room...it's the same as it was in the fifties."

Anticipations of the future were similar. "Not much anticipated." "It'll stay pretty much the same." "I'd say in ten years there'd be very little change." "Quite frankly, it will be just about the same." Some explained why there would be little change. We have already met the man who noted that past residents who had been here for "umpteen" years were now changing, but the new ones would be here for "umpteen" years. Others thought the residents themselves would contribute to preservation. "Everybody's interested in the same. A lot of people that live here are interested in preserving the way that it's been." The Millfield Society "is going to try to continue keeping Millfield similar to what it is."

There was some concern about change from outside forces, but also the expectation that those forces would be resisted. It isn't going to change unless "they tore down older houses and put up modern ones." Population is moving toward Millfield, "but there's no way for it to change unless they start cutting property down." "There's nowhere for it to go, really."

Most people did not want it to change; they liked it the way it is. "This is going to be the same old country village. And I hope it stays that way." Only one resident had reservations about lack of change. He felt the village was not changing because the county officials "don't want no progress."

Even those who did notice change were inclined to back off on its significance. An older resident who listed a whole series of changes having to do with the disappearance of businesses still thought "Millfield itself" had changed very little. Another who began by responding to the question affirmatively, "Yes, it sure has in every way, shape, and form," went on to list both physical and people changes only to conclude, "I don't think the community has really changed much in the way of a facelift from the last fifty years."

Only two anticipated future changes. One thought that people moving in from Coopertown would be more affluent and more likely to be owners than renters. The other feared the possibility of "rough neighborhoods" because "the kids now growing up" are "altogether a different breed."

The City at the Gates

One kind of apprehension about future change is that it will come from outsiders building malls or developments, destroying the surrounding beauty, and increasing traffic and noise. A man who apologized because he knew his yard was full of cars in various states of repair nevertheless worried that a development might appear in the cornfield across the street. He believes that a lot of people in Millfield share his concern. "That's the reason we moved out here, so we could see a cornstalk across....If we wanted to live in an upper-level development area, then we'd a moved there."

Others expressed concern about what would go into fields across from or behind their houses, or that there would be a gas station on the corner of Route 69, or that a mall might be built near Millfield. "That would, I think, have a big impact on traffic." One man envisioned Millfield surrounded by ranch houses. "Oh, definitely. That's right across the road from us. That's why I had four trees started in my backyard." His neighbor commented, "I'd hate to see a housing project or something built in that cornfield across the street." Another had an even more dire vision. "See, we are going to get a shopping center, there's plans for that. They are going to buy it and put up a factory...and bulldoze Millfield down. Factories are right up around us now, we are surrounded by factories and businesses..."

Traffic had been noted as an already existing problem, both passing on Route 69 and coming through the center of the village on Millfield Road. Residents referred to the increase in noise, traffic as a nuisance, traffic being "already terrible," and big trucks on Millfield Road going from Route 69 to the Brixton-Corinth Road, which leads into the Coopertown Center.

While most residents weren't worried about Millfield being bulldozed, there was considerable discussion about whether the ranch houses would actually appear in the village. One felt that a mall would increase traffic but "I don't know that it would change, you know, the neighborhood." Another agreed that Millfield wouldn't be much affected if the mall had an exit on the side away from the village. Others felt that new housing could surround Millfield but not enter it. But one man added, "unless they start cutting property down," and another woman thought there wouldn't be a change unless older houses were torn down. "I just don't foresee that," she added.

There was also apprehension that change could come about because of the incorporation of Millfield in Coopertown and a change in the nature of the governing body of that town. One man was concerned that the town might come in and "start making laws to do something about Millfield." He was worried about laws against chickens, ducks, and old cars. Another thought that the biggest change that had taken place was "the jurisdiction change." Her neighbor, a younger urbanite, also mentioned that Millfield was part of Coopertown, not like a village "that is actually isolated." When the questioner noted that the Millfield sign still marked an entrance to the village, she replied, "even if they take the sign out, we'll put another one up."

But she also looked at the change with an ambivalent perspective. The town council was changing from "little boys, very much rural southern Ohio" to "people associated with the university and with the base, who are more affluent." She was not saying this was better or worse, but "just that they're very, very different. And the older people, especially the people with Appalachian backgrounds...they don't like these new people coming in and taking over the water systems and all the things that these people demand...City planners, you know." This view of the town contrasted with that of a resident who worked for the county, which was probably still more rural in outlook. Any change you want to make "they're completely against it."

Only two households expressed any interest in the possibility of fighting malls or condominiums by participating in town politics, both of them younger, professional, more recent residents of Millfield. One older resident managed to cover almost all apprehensive possibilities: "You never know what's gonna come through, or what they're gonna do. You can't predict anything."

Absences are difficult to notice. Researchers usually worry over what is in their data rather than what is not. But anyone who had done any work on peace research knows that if you ask people, they will tell you that they are concerned about the possibility of nuclear war. When, however, we asked them about their expectations for the next ten years, on a sunny Saturday in October, not one person in any of the twenty-four households interviewed mentioned being worried in the slightest that Millfield might be destroyed in a nuclear disaster.

Actually, Millfield residents not only are unworried about nuclear war, but don't seem to be much worried about malls, condominiums, traffic, or zoning by the city council. Asked why they might leave Millfield, only the man who thought the village might be bulldozed indicated any possibility of being "forced out." But he went on to discuss who would inherit his property, so he did not seem seriously concerned about having to leave.

The most common response was that people didn't expect to move at all. "I figure we'll be here the rest of our lives." After retirement, "we'll still live here, 'cause I don't think you can find...any place cheaper than it is here." "They'd have to 'drag me out.' If you have a warm, comfortable, paid-for house, 'why move?'"

Of those who would move, most spoke of employment elsewhere, or the possibility of having to move for as yet nonexistent health reasons or because it would be too expensive to maintain a large house after the family had moved out and one had retired. Most of these speculations were accompanied by indications that the residents would prefer to remain in Millfield if they could.

Only in four of the households was there an indication of wanting to move. One family had already bought a retirement farm, and another planned to return to the husband's Tennessee home. One man said he would leave when he finds a seven-bedroom Victorian house with ten acres of ground and woods. Another couple that had always lived in or near Millfield allowed that they might move for "a place in the country—if we could afford it." "With a little bit of land...But not far away."

A Hint of Uneasiness

One of the most curious aspects concerning perceptions of social change in Millfield has to do with a battle that may or may not be taking place. Battle is much too strong a word: there isn't even a conflict, just a hint of uneasiness.

We began with a pretty good idea of what we thought was happening. What we thought was that young, urban professionals were moving in, buying houses in what they perceived to be a quaint community, perhaps fixing them up, and thereby threatening the older inhabitants with higher taxes and perhaps urban standards.

The first way we tried to demonstrate this (Chapter III) was by asking residents of the households why they moved to or remained in Millfield. We thought that the young, urban professionals would have moved in because they wanted a sense of community, whereas the older residents would be there because they liked the house they were in or because their families lived in the area. Sure enough, we got an even break on all of these items: Twelve of the twenty-four households mentioned community and twelve did not. Also twelve mentioned house and twelve mentioned family (obviously some mentioned more than one). We then checked to see if there would not be strong positive correlations between those who—unprompted—perceived community and the young, urban professionals. We checked for age, professional work, textbook grammar, a relatively short period of residence, those who came from outside Coopertown, and those with college educations. But the correlations were weak throughout. The young, urban professionals, by any measure we could think of, were no more likely than the old rural colloquials to perceive community in Millfield.

All the same, there does seem to be some ambivalence about younger people moving in and fixing up their houses. Six of the residents referred to younger people moving in. One man in his forties described them as "mostly young, and fairly well-educated or professionals."

How will these newer people affect the community? One thing they will do is fix up their houses. Residents of five different households referred to that. "I think that there are some people starting to buy and fix up homes now that the school house has been bought and they are working on that." "Hopefully there will be...more younger people get some of these old houses and fix them up. I'd like to see some of that." "The people that move in who want to preserve it as a small town." What possible objection could there be to that?

But there was an edge to some comments. "The newer people that's got in," said one man, "they're trying to change it to a, what is it?" "Historical," replied his wife. "Historical thing now," he said. Change it? From what to what? Another man commented a bit derisively that he thought Millfield would become "the best historical pop area."

His neighbor explained that he didn't want to see split levels or ranch houses built but "I'm not a big proponent of this historical village thing. I mean, I guess I'm kinda greedy. I like the best of two worlds." What two worlds? He had read in the village newspaper about "the Millfield Club wanting to try to get Millfield to become a historical village....If it doesn't put a hardship on everybody, then, ya know, I see nothing wrong with it....If it puts a stipulation on there that hey, I cannot add a room on the back of my house because it doesn't conform with the way the house was built and...it upsets the balance of how the homes look, then I think that's wrong. Because I think that's the American thing—that you should be able to do within limitations what you want to do."

Perhaps the most suggestive summary of the conflict was that in the past decade "types of people have changed, I don't know if its more education or what...they're trying to make it a historical village...I think the people that have lived here for years and years accept Millfield the way it was and I think there's a group here that wants to preserve it the way it is..." Was it a conflict, then, between a group that wants to restore it to as it was and a group that wants to preserve it as it is?

Was this a conflict about increased taxes because of improvements or possibly higher standards of appearance? We have referred to the man who worried that future zoning might prevent him from keeping chickens, or his neighbor from working on cars. Another saw the charm in Millfield of having one's housekeeping expectations sufficiently casual so that you would be comfortable with anyone dropping in at any time.

Was there a concern about liberal ideas coming in with these newcomers or perhaps even minority groups? One long-time resident commented on the only black family in the village. "Well it was all white until about ten years ago...we don't know how he got in here...He's real nice, you know." Could that be read, there's a black family, then, but only one, and they're really nice, so there has been no big change in that?

So there are hardly factions in Millfield. There is no clear-cut situation of young urbanites fixing up homes and imposing table manners and neatness on their country cousins. But there's just a bit of wariness that things might be preserved as they are rather than as they were.

What About Street Lights?

We thought that perhaps one aspect of this conflict would be city-type improvements like streetlights, sidewalks, and home-delivered mail. We thought the older, more colloquial residents would be more likely to want improvements of that type, and the newer, better-educated residents would want to do without those conveniences in order to preserve the community. It turned out that only four people referred to such changes, all of them long-time residents, but one of these opposed the changes. And many people of both types spoke favorably about the post office as a community center.

There were two people who were pro-streetlight, one pro-sidewalk, and one, heresy of heresies, anti-post office. One lady said she would like to have streetlights, seeing as Millfield was now part of Coopertown and presumably paying taxes for them. Another, on the same side street, also saw a need for more lighting and spoke favorably of her neighbor putting in sidewalks, "which the town should've done." The post-office "Scrooge" commented, "A lot of people, even the new residents in Millfield, like the quaintness and the thing of sayin', hey, I can go to the post office and get my mail, ya know. I guess they got it in the back of their minds that a New England farm town or somethin' and they're gonna take the sled down there and get the mail...I just as soon they deliver the mail to the front porch."

The one person who explicitly opposed added services was also an owner of an artesian well: "We don't want the water, if it comes through, which I didn't even want it."

Perceptions of History

We thought that the newer, better-educated people moving into Millfield would be more interested in its contextual history, its political and economic background, and also perhaps about the actual previous ownership of houses.

TABLE VII-1

Education and Length of Residency of Millfield Households (N=21)

	Education	Residence
More years	7	13
Fewer years	14	8
Total	21	21

They would have a greater stock of what was beyond memory, perhaps actually read some local history. We expected the older, less highly educated residents would have a better knowledge of oral history, direct memory of how things were, and how they have changed.

Among the twenty-four households, we received twenty-one replies on Millfield history. We related these replies to two variables: education and length of residence. Those households containing a person being interviewed

TABLE VII-2

Education and Length of Residency of Millfield Families (N=21)

More years residence, fewer years education	11
More years education, fewer years residence	5
More years education, more years residence	2
Fewer years residence, fewer years education	3

who had more than thirteen years of education we considered to have "more" education. We used thirteen rather than twelve as the dividing point because the two who had thirteen years of education seemed basically high school-educated in other contexts such as work and language.

We considered those who had lived in Millfield longer than a decade as having more years of residence and those who lived a decade or less having fewer years. Again, the one family with ten years of residence seemed in other contexts to be the earliest of the "new" residents. Using these criteria, we made Table VII-1 to describe the education and length of residence of the responding households.

The figures suggest that Millfield is not being inundated with new residents. It turned out that both the mean and median period of residence of the longest resident in each household was twenty-three years. So long-time residents seemed to constitute a solid majority by every kind of measure.

We thought that families with more years of education would tend to have fewer years of residence, and vice versa. That was more often, but not always, the case (Table VII-2).

Let's begin with political and economic history, since that would seem to be the kind of history you would read about, rather than hear about. Residents of five households referred to political history. One mentioned a dispute about whether the county seat should be in Millfield, Corinth, or another town. Two knew the building that had once housed the Dewsberry County Court. One believed Millfield had once been the county seat of Dewsberry County. Three of these had been long-time residents and only two had more education. One knew that an early resident became State Senator Wilson. So the anticipated pattern did not apply to political history.

Residents of eight households were familiar with Millfield's economic history. Two were familiar with its position as a regional transportation center. It was a central crossing for roads from Brixton, Corinth, and a town to the south. "I would have thought," said one resident, "that there had to be some kind of transportation through here for even the mill to have started." Another knew "it was one of the first communities in the area and that it had a lot to do with the railway station." A third referred to how heavy rail traffic used to be without evaluating the economic significance. The resident who mentioned Senator Wilson also knew that he built three factories that gave the name to nearby Ironmonger Road.

Several were aware of Millfield's decline as an economic community. "Basically it was a stock and grain community in the 1800s. There were two or three affluent people in the area. It was a quiet, little farming community." "You know when the railroads were the big thing...this was a thriving business community, but now its just a residential community." The closing of the mill signified the "transition from farm to urban. Coal was a big item twenty years ago. The grain elevator (the mill) was in operation until ten years ago." "Trucks needed to line up on that road in the summer time to get in through the elevator."

Once again, there was no strong correlation between education, length of residence, and information about economic history. Four of the eight had less education and five were long-time residents.

Regarding social history we would have expected more equality, since such information might be transmitted in writing or orally or might simply have been observed by long-time residents. The resident who had the most information was active in the Historical Society, had a college education, and was relatively a short-timer in residence: ten years. She mentioned a trolley from Brixton, a beach house, the railroad, the town grocery store, the route of the railroad to Corinth and the town to the south. "Millfield had a band at one time...would have been a pretty bustling place in the late 1800s." She mentioned a number of fires that burned down some business buildings and the woods that then surrounded the town.

Her kind of information seems quite different from that of the oldest resident interviewed, who described how the street car went through, how the mail was put down and picked up by the railroad train, and how, when Route 69 went through, it divided farmland so that farmers had to drive cattle across the road. She described how you could go to her husband's dad's grocery store "and buy penny candy crackers that come in these square boxes where you get 'em by the pound and the cookies the same way. They cut your meat like you wanted it, if you want steak they'd cut you a slab of steak and cheese the same way...My land! Sugar, you could go in there and buy sugar by the pound if you want. You dip it out of a great big thing."

Two others knew about major fires and one referred to the flood of 1959, which he experienced but no one else mentioned. The beach house was referred to nudgingly. Or was it the hotel? "The infamous Millfield Hotel." The dance hall was a trysting place. "There's that house. I'm sure you heard about that, ha?"

The trolley also was noted by another. "Used to be a traction stop, when the traction car ran out, came from Brixton.... People rode the traction cars to dances at the dance halls." And one woman remembered that when she first moved in, there used to be outhouses in the backyards and houses didn't have heat upstairs. This sort of information came from eight households, equally divided on the amount of education, with six of the eight having members who had lived longer than a decade in Millfield.

So knowledge of political, economic, and social history did not prove to be an exclusive province of the better-educated who had moved into Millfield more recently.

We thought the better-educated newcomers might know more about particular histories, the ownership of particular houses. The long-time residents would be more likely to remember changes in businesses or uses of buildings.

Residents of eight houses provided information of this sort. Three mentioned the closing of the grain elevator or mill, and four mentioned the disappearance of grocery or confectionery stores. Three, including the present owner, mentioned the closing of a slaughterhouse: "I know this (house) was a store. The portion on the side was a meat market, I should say, and the slaughterhouse was out in the back."

One mentioned that "Chester Puckett's Antiques" used to be the "Old Stage Coach Inn, but perhaps that isn't Millfield." The old Coopertown Schoolhouse was mentioned two or three times, but only once in response to the historical question. Older post offices were mentioned a couple of times as were the hotel, beach house, and dance hall.

Besides the owner of the slaughterhouse, a few others mentioned their own house or houses adjacent. One knew that his own house and the house next door used to be warehouses belonging to Millfield Seed and Grain. Another knew her house was nearly one hundred years old, "one of the oldest in Millfield."

There was not much knowledge of ownership. One man volunteered: "These two brick houses were supposed to have been built by two daughters." "I think that's pretty much a fact," added his wife. As mentioned, one resident knew a big house either just in or just out of Millfield was built by Wilson, the factory owner. Only one pair of residents reported past names connected with their own house. They had bought the house from the Barnets, who had bought it from a man named Rittenhouse, who served in the legislature in the nineteenth century. He bought it from a man named Arbon, who built it around 1860. More information was provided about changing businesses than houses, but what there was had little relation to years of education or residence.

Did the newer residents have a better contextual history? Did they know more beyond personal memory or more that had a context of history beyond the particular building or house? Information of that sort would include knowledge of the relationships of the grain mill and the railroad to the surrounding area, views on the kind of community Millfield was in the nineteenth century, knowledge of conflict in the area over the location of the county seat, knowledge of the nineteenth century fires, and knowledge of early people.

And here one difference emerges. All seven people with college educations had a long-term historical knowledge, while only five of the fourteen with fewer years of education did. And four of those with more education, all of them recent arrivals, had contextual knowledge of Millfield's history, while none of those with fewer years of education did. This seems to be the one difference in historical perception, but it does seem striking.

Good Old Days

We thought the appearance of younger, better-educated immigrants might affect perceptions of past and future in another way. Older residents would prefer the past and think the present and future less appealing. Newer residents would be more optimistic about the future.

The "good old days" perception was presented by a resident who remarked, "You know, people before, they used to help each other, but the people today, you just can't find people that's willing to help." Another notes several changes for the worse. "That kind of stuff[the mail and milk pickups] is gone. We kind of miss it." And Hickory Street, for instance, "was beautiful when I lived down there. It's run down since we lived there."

A short-time resident, married to a long-time resident, mildly regretted changes he had not witnessed. "You know, when the railroads were the big thing...this was a thriving business community, but now it's just a residential community...It didn't go from bad to worse, as far as its economical condition, it went from good to bad." One short-time resident was concerned about a possible increase in rentals while a long-time resident thought rentals were declining. Both agreed ownership was preferable to rentals.

Three not very long-time residents (eight to fourteen years) regretted the increase in traffic both on Millfield Road and Gateway Route 69. One long-time resident anticipated a decline because of the nature of the children now growing up in Millfield—"a different breed." Others noted improvements. One long-time resident felt the decline in trains was an improvement: "Used to be a nuisance...it's no longer because they don't run like they used to."

Three newer residents living near each other agreed that more people were moving in and fixing up their houses. Another remarked more generally that in the past two years, "there seems to be more awareness of one's surroundings and trying to change things for the better."

Both the "good old days" and the "change for the better" themes were muted. There was much more emphasis on how Millfield had changed and would change very little. And those who recalled lost virtues of the past were committed to living out their lives in Millfield and had no expectations of moving elsewhere.

People and Things

When people do see change, are they more likely to focus on changes in people or things? We thought things, particularly changes in buildings, would be more visible. This proved to be the case. Changes in things were mentioned in seventeen households, changes in people in only ten.

Changes in things included the disappearance or change in uses of buildings, removal of railway tracks, increase in traffic, houses becoming run down, and paving. Changes in people include new faces, increased awareness, more education, less willingness to help, deaths of older citizens, and younger families. People fixing up their houses seem to be a combination of both.

In this case there was an interesting difference in the relation between memories and both education and residence. Of the thirteen with a long period of residence who responded, all thirteen remembered changes in things, but only five noted changes in people. Those with short residence were inclined to notice both. Four of five noted changes in things, all noted changes in people.

Recapitulation

Our first expectation, that people would be more likely to perceive change in the past than the present, was not confirmed. On the whole they were inclined to perceive that Millfield had changed very little and would change very little, even though a number of them also made statements that indicated they were aware of considerable historical change.

While statements were found indicating that some residents regretted losses of symbols or personal relationships, this theme was muted compared with the perception that things had not changed very much; and the three long-time residents who made the strongest statements about the superiority of certain aspects of the past indicated that they hoped and expected to live out their lives in Millfield.

The expectation that there might be a conflict between better-educated newcomers and residents who had lived in Millfield for a longer period was not supported, but it could be said that there is some recognition of a difference and some uneasiness about it. Newcomers and long-time residents had about an equal sense of community, but the newcomers seem more eager that people fix up their houses, while older residents seem concerned that standards of preservation could reach a level and intensity that would prevent them from doing things they want to do, force them to do things they don't want to do, or perhaps just change the atmosphere of the community, making it more formal, less homey.

The expectation that long-time residents would be more interested in and less resistant to urban improvements was very mildly supported. Most residents did not refer to such changes at all.

The expectation that the newcomers would have a different kind of perception about the history of Millfield was only mildly supported. By several kinds of criteria, there seemed to be little difference. It did appear that the newcomers were more likely to have a contextual sense of history, but they were not more likely than long-term residents to possess information about political, economic, or social history or about history beyond the memory of the living residents.

Our expectation was confirmed that concern about the influences of the expanding urban area on the village would be widely shared. The concern was frequent and various. At the same time, also as expected, residents either did not expect that their worries would be realized or that, if they were, Millfield would still be Millfield. One indication of this was that no one expected to leave Millfield because of anticipated changes in the village.

On the whole, then, the residents of this village at the edge of an expanding metropolitan area expect that it will continue to be what it is—a small, quiet, bucolic community of older homes. They worry about external changes but do not think they will have a major impact. The long-time residents are concerned about differences in the newcomers, but they do not anticipate that they will bring about really significant change.

Chapter VIII

Millfield on Saturday

Millfield as a Community Model

What then, have we learned from visiting Millfield on Saturday?

Certainly, in terms of the *Gemeinschaft-Gessellschaft* dichotomy, there is plenty of both. If you are considering symbols and images or feelings of peace and satisfaction, Millfield delivers for its residents. If you think, on the other hand, that Millfield is just a launching pad for daily and weekend activities that occupy the inhabitants, there is plenty of evidence that this is the case.

The community image that everybody knows everybody is, of course, exaggerated by any measure. If you interpret the image as meaning that people walking to the post office can usually identify other people as belonging or not belonging to the community, that may well be the case in a high percentage of instances. If you mean when one person sees another, he knows where she lives, that would be true in more like 37 percent of encounters. If you mean one would perceive another as a close friend, that would probably be so on fewer than one meeting in ten.

On the other hand, the community is hardly in eclipse. It is difficult to compare it to what it was before Brixton and Coopertown expanded to the Gates, or even to a town like Springdale, because comparative data are not available. But there is plenty of evidence for belief in the community and for measures of interaction that show that people actually do walk to the post office to pick up their mail and talk to others on the streets, on the lawns, and on the porches, to rescale a Churchillian metaphor.

Another military metaphor already referred to, the launching pad, also has validity, though launching pad really understates the case. While at any given time Millfield appears tranquil, with perhaps one car to be seen leaving or entering at a very modest pace, a diagram of a Friday and Saturday would reveal a very different picture, with a beehive perhaps providing a more appropriate metaphor, with the busy bees of Millfield leaving in great numbers for work, for visits to relatives, on helping missions, trips to the Grange, restaurants, football games, or malls.

One measure of stability suggested in the literature is length of residence. If people have lived in the community for a long period of time, they will know more people and help provide stability. If people move in and out frequently, the neighborhood will be less stable. But would a neighborhood like Millfield, by appearing to be desirable, upset its own stability? Would the demand for housing increase, the value of houses go up, and by the influx of new residents would the stability decrease?

Apparently not. In fifteen of the twenty-four households interviewed, residents had lived in the community ten years or more, with the median residence being fourteen years. Despite concern about newcomers, expressed very cautiously by a few residents, rapid turnover does not seem to be following the apparent desired ability of the community. If residence in Millfield appears more desirable to outsiders, it must appear so to insiders as well.

Another criterion is the ratio between owners and renters, with degree of ownership being associated with safety and stability. If so, Millfield had nothing to fear, with twenty-three of the twenty-four households interviewed being owned by occupants. The one exception involved a young couple very much concerned about and involved in the life of the community.

Were there urban nomads sweeping into the community, buying houses at inflated rates, and forcing up taxes so that decent folk would have to move out? It didn't appear so. There was concern on the part of some of the decent folk that newcomers, the proponents of the Millfield Historical Society, might pose a future danger to the ducks of the community. But for the present, the ducks appeared to be safe.

The uneasiness about the Historical Society reflected a historical conflict in community literature. We want our community to be safe and friendly, but we also want to be free to go about our business. Millfielders feel that the community is safe because people keep an eye on things, know a stranger when one appears, but at the same time, they don't want to be intruded upon, to be free to come and go without questions being raised.

The literature of community is much involved with the definition of neighborhood. Should it be defined as a certain area created by "natural" boundaries or landmarks, or should it be defined by networks of acquaintance? It turned out that Millfield could be defined both ways. Visually, it appeared to be one big neighborhood, and many people thought it was, but as you got your bearings, you became aware of subdivisions defined by area. Once these areas were perceived, it could be shown that there were corresponding networks or, preferably, circles of acquaintance. But it also turned out that neighborhoods could be defined by circles of acquaintance, with area taken only as a secondary consideration. For Millfield, either approach produced distinctive neighborhoods within the community.

Perception of Community

We had expected that people moving into Millfield from other areas of Brixton might be more interested in the community than those who had been there a long time. They might, we thought, be somewhat inclined to romanticize it.

Our interviews revealed nothing of the sort. It was true that some residents referred to the charm, the beauty, the ambiance of Millfield as a reason for choosing to live there, while an equal number made no such reference and spoke in terms of the house, the location, the basement, the corner cupboard, or other factors that seemed to ignore the community itself. But we could find no correlation between the presence or absence of community references and the length of time people had lived there. Living a long time in Millfield did not seem to dull the sense of charm; moving in recently did not seem to sharpen the perception.

Attempts to establish other relationships between perception of community and background produced no strong correlations. People who came from the city did not have a stronger perception than people who came from rural areas; people with more years of education or textbook grammar did not have a stronger perception than people with fewer years or colloquial grammar. Occupation, age, or gender did not strongly relate to perception. Community was as evident to the labor or service occupied person as it was to the manager, professional, or homemaker.

It would appear, then, that Millfield's community is appreciated by many residents, more by some than others. The community is pleasant, but not overwhelming, not the central factor in anyone's life.

Image and Activity

What was the image of community? Millfielders see their village as a friendly place where people walk around, greet one another, chat in the front yards, feel safe, trust one another, help and look out for each other, but can also relax and feel at peace without having their privacy invaded—a charming, enjoyable place to live, a pretty little place surrounded by nature.

The activities of people over the weekend would not destroy the image. If a person never greeted or helped anyone all day long, that would not prove that he/she did not do so on other days. If one thinks he/she is at peace, one hundred sociologists with ten thousand pages of counter evidence wouldn't really disturb the peace.

But if the image is valid, we would expect it to be reinforced in some ways, and in many ways it is. People do congregate at the post office. Many people did spend time relaxing, doing nothing. Not one interview was interrupted by anyone having to rush off elsewhere.

On the whole, however, Millfielders were not doing many of the things they thought they did. On the Saturday of the interview, no one mentioned helping anyone doing anything else, or being helped by anyone. And two who were sick received no chicken soup that day. Perhaps such events were so taken for granted that the interaction would not be considered worth mentioning. The beauty of the community must also be spontaneous, for the perception of the couple working on their house that many others were doing the same thing was not confirmed. No one else was working on the house. If people were watching out for strangers, it didn't get back to the strangers who were interviewing, though there was evidence that the word was around about who we were.

Encounters with neighbors at the post office were not mentioned, though again this could be so routine that it was not perceived as an "activity." The auction, supposedly a central event in the community, was mentioned only by two people.

Safety and trust were hard to measure. We didn't ask if people locked their doors when they engaged in various activities. Beauty and charm, mill and cornfields could all be observed. But they were a given, Grace if you will, not something anyone was doing anything about, maintaining, or improving.

Privacy was hard to measure, but it was true that in no interview was anyone present who was not a member of the household.

The launching pad metaphor was well confirmed. Millfielders left the village in double digit numbers to go to work, to school, and to buy goods or services: groceries, garage sale items, restaurant meals and entertainment, including football games, drag races, and park strolls. But no one played golf and no one was going to a movie, play, symphony performance, or ballet, so the advantages of being near Brixton were not being used. People also left in great numbers to visit relatives, either to socialize or to help with some kind of project. Only one couple, active in the VFW, was socializing with people who were not relatives, though another mentioned that visiting a nearby restaurant on Saturday morning included catching up on local gossip.

An equal amount of time was spent in Millfield, but the activities had little to do with Millfield images, except for relaxing, which was practiced creatively in the form of sleeping, showering, watching television, or doing nothing. Most of the work done was routine, the kind anyone would do anywhere: caring for children, house cleaning, laundry, preparing meals, "odds and ends." In terms of Millfield images, however, the only activities mentioned that would relate to the image were stripping and sanding floors, sawing wood, and cleaning fish. The wood sawing, however, was for family outside of Millfield, and the fish cleaning reversed an image: the husband cleaning the fish his wife had caught.

There were, however, neighborly relations to be discerned. Members of half the households did mention walking in the community: Three walked to the post office, three mentioned specific neighborly encounters, two mentioned visiting the post office, and one was visited while working on his car by buddies who may or may not have been from Millfield.

One curious finding, not at all anticipated in the images, should bear further study. Apparently members of all twenty-four households in the sample spent at least some part of their Saturday being interviewed by visiting sociologists. There is nothing in the images or the literature to indicate that such activity is so widespread in American communities. Other studies will be needed to determine whether there was some special reason for this activity in Millfield or whether it is an activity that occurs widely in such communities around the nation.

Neighbors and Family

The secondary role of friendships, apparent in the identification of best friends within the community, was supported by the Millfielders observations about their community. Neighborhood relations were perceived as casual. You greeted people, chatted, or shared a beer, but did not invite one another into your house. Community affairs brought people together, but these occurred only a few times a year.

There is no doubt that Millfielders perceived the village as a single community. Anyone would be friendly to anyone else in a street encounter. But it turned out that the people who actually walked across the lawn to talk to others on porches were likely to live in the same neighborhood. Anecdotes about jokes or borrowing involved neighbors. If there was any perception of division in the community, it involved the Historical Society, and that turned out to have an area basis too, with most of the members living along Millfield Road in central or south Millfield and most of those who considered themselves excluded living on Hickory Street.

If the neighborhoods provided a general supportive background for social interactions, families were central in those interactions. All but four of the households had kin living within an hour of the village and more than half encountered these relatives at least once a week. On the Saturday in question, people spent a considerable amount of time visiting or being visited by relatives and described these encounters with considerable zest. But members of nine households also mentioned outside recreational activity with friends.

Half the households mentioned various nuclear family activities taken outside the village, as well as staying home and gardening with other members of the family or taking care of children. Generally, specific activities with family or friends were more vividly described; relations with neighbors were more casual.

Neighborhoods

The image of Millfield as a single community was contradicted by perceptions that there were several distinct geographical areas even within so small a community. It was clear that everyone did not "know" everyone in Millfield to the extent that each knew where each lived in the whole community, though it is possible that those who went to the post office would recognize others who did the same or would know who was seen on porches or lawns along the way.

Millfielders could identify the occupants of more households in their own area-defined neighborhoods than they could in others, and this was true for each of the four neighborhoods. So the areas did have some validity in terms of familiarity.

But it also turned out that Millfielders knew more people who lived nearby than farther away, up to a certain distance. That distance turned out to be a 1000 feet, about a fifth of a mile. Beyond that distance the relationship between distance and knowing was reversed. This somewhat undercut the neighborhood idea since, on the whole, people in your own neighborhood would also live nearer by, so what appeared to be a function of clustering pattern could be a function of distance.

The distance factor was somewhat supported when it turned out that people were more familiar with where others lived in adjacent neighborhoods than they were in neighborhoods that were separated by another neighborhood.

Was there any validity to the post office image? If people walking to the post office really did chat with people who lived in the houses along the way, wouldn't it be likely that they would be more familiar with where people lived on the route to the post office than in the other direction? We were able to chart that, and it turned out they were more familiar with homes of those who lived on the route.

So area-defined neighborhoods, distance, and the post office all seemed to play a part in influencing the extent to which people knew where other people lived. (Historian Carl Becker, who grew up in Miamisburg, Ohio, mentions that an evening game he played with an old fellow resident consisted of one naming a street address and the other trying to recall who lived there.)

But the community literature says, and we ourselves endorsed the idea in Chapter II, that neighborhoods ought to be identified by networks of acquaintance, not by geographically defined areas. Once we had transformed the networks to circles we were able to identify such neighborhoods by individuals and by the area neighborhoods themselves. This method produced neighborhoods that looked different, with considerable overlap among three of the four. From this perspective we were able to find justification for consolidating the overlapping neighborhoods and calling Millfield a community with two acquaintance-determined neighborhoods or four area-determined neighborhoods. But geography still played a part, and it turned out that the accident of four neighboring households with a relatively low level of household familiarity may have been responsible for the division of familiarity that undercut the image that Millfield was one big community with no neighborhood divisions. So it was possible to define neighborhoods by familiarity, but this could not be divorced from geographical relationships.

Among other factors considered, education did not seem to have much relation to familiarity, but length of residence did. In Millfield it would appear that in five years of residence you would know half the people you would ever know in the community, but the number increased until thirty years of residence. After that, it declined, perhaps because of a decline in activity. Being known by others, however, never declined.

Friendships played a less important part in the community than acquaintance. Fewer than 10 percent of acquaintances were defined as among a resident's three best friends. The view that the community provides general support for living without being a center of friendship was supported by the Millfielders identification of acquaintances and friends.

On the whole, the image of the community as the mellow background from which specific activities with family or friends were undertaken was repeated whether you were considering people's perceptions, their activities, or their acquaintance patterns. Except that the supportive community background was more likely to come from the neighborhood.

Past and Future

Finally, we considered perceptions of past and future. Had Millfield changed? Was it changing? We thought there would be a good deal of reminiscing about the good old days, with unfavorable comparisons of present to past. There was some, but the dominant view was that Millfield had not changed all that much, at least as compared to the greater Brixton area, and that it was likely to continue resisting change.

There were fears for the future. Among older residents there was some muted concern that newcomers, members of the Historical Society, might try to revive the past, and in so doing raise the standards, imposing difficulties for older residents. But on the whole, the expectation seemed to be that zoning laws, condominiums in the cornfields, the aspirations of newcomers, the federal government, or nuclear war would not very much affect Millfield. It would continue to be what it was, *sans* sidewalks, streetlights, and mail delivery.

Those Early Questions

In Chapters I and II some questions were raised about Millfield that had their origins either in the authors' wildest imaginations as the survey was being prepared or out of the theories of some of the past giants of community studies. The time has come to reconsider these questions, whether to see if we have become wiser in some ways or to admit ignorance in areas where our inquiry has cast little light. It may be that we must respond as Dodgers to some of the problems of the Giants.

There were, for instance, a set of preliminary hypotheses in Chapter I. Let us see how they fared.

Those supported were:

1. Social networks were stronger for most people, in terms of interaction and intensity, outside of Millfield rather than inside.
2. The majority of Millfielders are immigrants from some other Ohio community.
7. Greater Brixton and Corinth networks with Millfield were probably more numerous than Coopertown-Millfield networks.
12. Kinship relationships were not strikingly different between long- and short-term residents of Millfield.

13. Most Millfielders did not expect to move.
15. Nearby people were better known than those living farther away, but were not central in a friendship network.
16. Activities concerned work, household, kin, and outside affairs to a greater extent than community.

Hypotheses not supported were:
3. Charm wasn't usually the first reason for buying a home in Millfield.
4. and 5. Millfield was neither favored as a place to live nor promoted as a community more by women than by men.
8. Immigrants were not bigger Millfield boosters than natives or long-time residents.
9. Long-time residents remembered community activities of the past with pleasure, but also spoke favorably about present activities.
14. Most Millfielders did not see others as having closer community relationships than they did themselves.

And there were three hypotheses that could not be answered from our data. We don't know

6. about Millfield as a favorable or unfavorable location with reference to work;
10. if family networks are as strong today as they were twenty-five years ago; and
11. how Millfield divorce rates compare to those of greater Brixton.

In Chapter II on community theory, we closed with a section entitled, "What About Millfield?" Many of the questions raised in that section have been addressed along the way, but it might provide a different insight to put them together.

Is Millfield a Wirthian community? Despite neighborhoods, it seems so. But we also see that neighbors usually are neither friends nor family. Among neighbors some are better known than others and closer neighbors are likely to have closer relations, though they are rarely intimate. It is difficult to say from our data how much difference it makes whether there are children in the family. But there seem to be no nighdwellers. Even those who thought of themselves as isolated could usually identify community members from at least half a dozen households. Do local facilities such as the post office play an important role? Apparently, the post office does, but there seems to be no other such facility unless it was the informal garage where the young male adults met.

Millfield turned out to be not very self-contained, with people leaving many times for many reasons in the two days we asked about. Still, there seems to be a good case for calling it a place of refuge. People did a great deal of puttering, relaxing, resting, and sleeping.

We couldn't measure the effect of home ownership, since all but one of the households interviewed included a homeowner. But it would be hard to call Millfield a community of limited liability. There is very little social organization, but then there are few social problems. The community is maintained very informally, perhaps supported by the image. To some extent it is what it seems, because people think it is. They are trusting, for instance, and therefore trust is reinforced.

We did not find that urbanites have more outside relationships than longer-established villagers. Millfielders in general seem to have extended networks outside the village.

There did not seem to be a decline in neighborhood solidarity. Residents remember the good old days and see some evidence of decline, but when they talk about the present, friendly community relationships are what they perceive. The newcomers have been noticed and are a source of mild anxiety, but the prevailing opinion seemed to be that their influence would either be beneficial or unimportant. There was some evidence that residents who moved in more recently had greater interest in improving the community by improving houses, but there was less evidence that many people were actually doing any improving. Millfield was hardly experiencing a process of gentrification.

Many of our questions, posed dramatically by theorists, had undramatic answers. There seem to be only minor differences between long-term and recent residents, nothing much that anyone would notice in those terms. The conflicts we look for between community and freedom scarcely existed, because community presumed freedom. And while social issues such as Coopertown zoning requirement were in the minds of a few, there was no dominant social issue in Millfield on Saturday.

Is Millfield what it appears to be, a Park and Burgess neighborhood, a neighborhood such as Shils described? Well, Shils' description as a summary of Millfield isn't far off the mark. Let's recall the quotation that ended Chapter II.

> To live in a district in which one feels "at home," to have neighbors, even if they are not friends, who greet one and offer a friendly smile is good. It may not appear to be a massive fact of social structure but it does have something to do with the satisfaction which a human being gets out of life. It might not integrate directly into the national community and it might have nothing to do with "goals." But not everything that human beings do has "goals." The good

may lie in the action itself, such as smiling, saying "Good Evening," chatting a few words about the weather or some other inconsequential subject. (Shils, 1980; quoted by Olson, 1982)

What Millfield Seems

It would seem, then, that in many ways Millfield is what it seems to be. It is a quiet place, a charming place, and the quiet and charm are appreciated by the residents. It is a community of people who are familiar with one another, who are comfortable, unhurried. At the same time, it is not an intrusive community. Privacy is protected partly because members of the community are not usually friends or family, and therefore, relationships can be pleasant without becoming intense.

Partly, the image does support the reality. We can show that on Saturday people spent as much time out of the community as in it, more time with family and friends than with neighbors, and that they really didn't make any soup for one another. But their belief that they can trust their neighbors, call upon them if in need, and their belief that it is a place of peace and refuge does contribute to making it all those things. They have trust, support, and peace mostly because they believe they have.

We can also show, and have had a great deal of fun showing, that Millfield, any way you look at it, is hardly one big community. It has neighborhoods defined by area or by circles of familiarity. Still, the legend of the post office can be empirically verified and, regardless of exact knowledge of where others live, the perception of community does define that community. The inhabitants of the two most distant houses may not know where each other live, but they probably recognize one another when they occasionally pass at the post office, and if a member of either household should find herself passing the house of the other, she would have no doubt that she was still in Millfield, not in Kansas.

Analogies to class struggle or to gentrification seem feeble. The rate of turnover is too slow and the people moving in are not sufficiently different in education, outlook, or wealth, not to mention race. No massive transformation appears to be in prospect; no one is likely to be driven out by tax increases, though it is possible one or two would leave because the sale price of a house proved to be attractive.

What Millfield lacks may be significant. There is no government to be taken over by college-educated town attorneys. There is no grocery store to be expanded into a supermarket. There is no route from anywhere to anywhere that could be widened to four lanes. Millfield has had a successful bypass operation of which the inhabitants were only faintly aware. The cornfields may fall to condominiums or, more likely, to brick ranch houses on an acre of land characteristic of the rest of Coopertown. But even were that to happen, the ranch houses would provide a similar monotonous background to cornfields, and Millfield would be as distinctive as ever.

If you like ranch houses on an acre of land, Millfield does no harm. If you don't, there is hope in the many charming villages that are facing encroachment by the city. You can move into them and become a citizen. In five years, you can know half the people you will ever know. And you can be accepted for what you are, even if you should happen to be a bearded sociologist. And peace and quiet, friendliness and trust may be had rather close to your office, the theater, and a good delicatessen.

And if you want to buy a couple of ducks, you need not fear the weird swishing sound that accompanies the mass raising of eyebrows.

Appendix

The Millfield Survey

MILLFIELD STUDY,   ADDRESS

COVER SHEET   I.D. #

Introduction. Hello, my name is Dr. _____ from Wright State University. I am conducting research here in Millfield with my colleagues. Your household has been randomly selected to participate. We would greatly appreciate the opportunity to talk to you about Millfield as a place to live. It is important for the scientific validity of our study that we are able to interview all the households chosen for the sample. May I have about a half hour of your time to ask you some questions?

(If YES) Thank you. May I come in? Before I begin let me assure you that anything you tell me will be kept in strictest confidence. At no time will you be personally identified, nor will anyone other than myself know what you say. This study is being conducted under strict ethics guidelines required and enforced by Wright State University. Do you have any questions? OK, let's begin.

(If NO) Let me just say two things before you make up your mind. First, anything you say will be kept in strictest confidence. At no time will you be personally identified, nor will anyone besides myself know what you have said. Second, while I realize my request may be inconvenient right now, it is very important that each of the households randomly chosen be included in this study. Failure to complete interviews with every household can seriously damage the accuracy of the study. If now is not a convenient time, could you spare some time later today? What about next Saturday, could I schedule an appointment with you then? Isn't there some time next week that we could get together? I'm sorry your viewpoints will not be represented in the study. Thank you for considering my request. Would you mind telling me if there is any particular reason (other than time) that you do not wish to be interviewed? It will help us to better evaluate the research design we are using for the study.

Interview results: (Check one)
[ ] Interview completed   [ ] No one home   [ ] Residence unoccupied
[ ] Interview refused   [ ] Interviewed   [ ] Respondent not capable
                              rescheduled

Time _____

Millfield Interview

I. Residential History
1. Let's begin by talking about when you first moved to Millfield. How long ago did you move here? (Check one)
    ( ) have lived here all life.
        (Go to question Q. 2)
    ( ) ___ years (Actual #)
   1a. Had you (or your spouse) ever lived in Millfield before?
    ( ) No (Go to Q. 4)
    ( ) Yes (Go to Q. 1b)
   1b. When was that? _____ (Go to Q. 4)
2. What are some of the reasons you stayed here?
   (Which have been most important?)
3. What have been some of the most important ways that Millfield has changed since your childhood here?

Are there any other changes that are particularly meaningful to you? (Go to Q. 7)
4. Where did you live before you moved here?
5. What were your reasons for moving here? (Which of these were the most important reasons?)
6. Has Millfield changed in any important way since you moved here?
7. Overall, how satisfied are you with Millfield as a place to live?

    ( ) Very Satisfied   ( ) Somewhat Dissatisfied

    ( ) Somewhat Satisfied   ( ) Dissatisfied

8. When you think of Millfield ten years from now, do you think it will be a better place to live, pretty much the same, or a worse place? (PROBE: WHY?)
9. What circumstances might get you to consider leaving Millfield?

II. Respondent's Household Characteristics. (Use summary chart below)

Now would you please tell me a little about the members of your household?

10. Including yourself, how many persons reside in your household? (If more than 1, go to Q. 10a)

   10a. Are you related to any of these persons?

      ( ) No (Go to Q. 11)

      ( ) Yes (If yes, go to 10b)

   10b. What is the relationship?

11. What is the age of each household member?
12. (If necessary) Is this person a male or female?
13. Are any members employed part time or full time?

      ( ) No (Go to Q. 14)

      ( ) Yes (If yes, go to Q. 13a)

13a. Who would that be and where are they employed?

Q. 10	Q. 10a	Q. 11	Q. 12	Q. 13	Q. 13a.
# HH	Relationship	Age	Gender	Employment	Place of Employment
1.					
2.					
3.					
4.					
5.					
6.					

14. Are you renting or do you own your residence? ( ) Rent ( ) Own

III. I would like to ask you some more questions about Millfield as a place to live.
- 15. Do you know much about the history of Millfield? For example,
  - a. What about important events that have affected the community?
  - b. Do you know much about certain buildings or houses such as previous owners or usage?
- 16. What kind of community do you think other people in this area think Millfield is?
  - 16a. Is it seen as better, about the same, or not as good a place to live?
  - 16b. Do people think of Millfielders as being a certain type of person?
- 17. a. What social groups and organizations do you know of here in Millfield?
  - b. Are there any cliques?
  - c. What about neighborhoods, does Millfield have any, or is it just

one big neighborhood?
18. Do you belong to any of the groups you have mentioned? (If no, WHY NOT?)
19. Are there social groups/organizations you belong to locally that are not in Millfield? (If yes, WHICH ONES?)
20. Here is a map of Millfield's homes. We would like for you to name as many of the individuals/families as you can who reside in these houses.
21. Would you consider any of these persons to be one of your three best friends? (If so, please circle those individuals on the map.)
22. Let's talk about your neighbors, that is the people living nearby.

    22a. Do you have much to do with your neighbors?

    22b. How much do you talk to, visit with, and help out one another?

    22c. Would you say that this is typical of most neighbors in Millfield? (If not, how is it different?)

IV. Kinship Interaction

Now we would like to ask you a few questions about your family.

23. Do you have any relatives who live in Millfield? (IF SO, go to 23a)

    23a. Who would that be?

24. Do you have relatives in the Greater Brixton area? That is within an hour's drive of you? (IF SO, go to 24a)

    24a. Who would that be?

    24b. In a typical month about how often do you see any of these relatives? Would you say you see someone,

        ( ) Several times a week

        ( ) About once a week

        ( ) Less than once a week

        ( ) Less than once a month

25. Which relative(s) do you see the most?
26. (IF RESPONDENT HAS FAMILY IN HOUSEHOLD) In your family, would you say that you spend most of your free time doing things together, or does everyone have their own individual activities? What

kinds of things are you most likely to do together?

V. Community Activities

These next few questions are about activities that bring people together here in Millfield.

27. When and where are you most likely to meet and talk to other residents during the course of a typical day?
28. Are there any special events or activities that bring Millfield residents together? (What would they be?) (IF NO, GO TO Q. 30)
29. How do you feel about such activities? Do you look forward to them, not care one way or the other, or avoid them? Why?

VI. Finally, we are interested in how Millfield fits into your usual day-to-day activities.

30. For example, what about yesterday? Can you briefly run through what your day was like?

30a. What did you do during the morning?

30b. What about in the afternoon?

30c. In the evening?

31. How about today? What are your plans?

31a. Morning

31b. Afternoon

31c. Evening

VII. The last thing we would like you to tell us is your (IF MARRIED, and spouses) occupation and the amount of formal schooling that you have completed.

32. Occupation   R: _____   S: _____
33. Education   R: _____   S: _____

This completes our interview questions. Is there anything else you would like to say about Millfield? Anything you think we should know about this community?

We greatly appreciate you taking the time to help us. I hope you have enjoyed the interview. When we complete our study we will be happy to send you a summary as I said earlier, your remarks will be kept strictly confidential and in no way will be personally identified.

BIBLIOGRAPHY

Banfield, Edward. *The Unheavenly City.* Boston: Little Brown, 1968.

Birch, David L., et al. T*he Community Analysis Model.* U.S. Office of Policy Development and Research, 1979.

Bott, Elizabeth. F*amily and Social Networks.* Travistock, 1957, 1972, 2nd ed. Free Press.

Caplan, Gerald and Marie Killilea. *Support Systems and Mutual Aid.* Grune and Stratton, 1976.

Effrat, Marcia. *The Community.* Free Press, 1974.

Feagin, J. R. "Community Disorganization: Some Critical Notes." *Social Inquiry* 43 (1973): 123–46.

Firey, Walter I. M*an, Mind and Land.* Greenwood (1978, 1960 Reprint).

Fischer, Claude S. T*o Dwell Among Friends: Personal Networks in City and Town.* Chicago: Univeristy of Chicago Press, 1982.

____. *The Urban Experience.* New York: Harcourt Brace, 1984.

Flanagan, William G. U*rban Sociology: Images and Structure.* Allyn and Bacon, 1990.

Foley, Donald. N*eighbors or Urbanites?* University of Rochester, 1952.

Galster, George. H*omeowners and Neighborhood Investment.* Duke University Press, 1987.

Gans, Herbert J. T*he Urban Villagers.* Free Press, 1962.

Guest, A. M. and B. A. Lee. "The Social Organization of Local Areas." U*rban Affairs Quarterly* 19 (1983): 217–40.

Gusfield, J. R. C*ommunity: A Critical Response.* New York: Harper and Row, 1975.

Hall, Edward G. B*eyond Culture.* New York: Doubleday, 1976.

Hannertz, Ulf. E*xploring the City.* Columbia University Press, 1980.

Hunter, Albert. "The Loss of Community: An Empirical Test Through Replication." *American Sociological Review* 40 (1975): 537–52.

Janowitz, Morris. *The Community Press in an Urban Setting*. Free Press, 1951.

Jones, T. J. *The Sociology of a New York City Block*. New York: Macmillan, 1904.

Kasarda, John D. and Morris Janowitz. "Community Attachment in Mass Society." *American Sociological Review* 39 (1974): 328–39.

Litwak, E. and J. Szelenyi. "Primary Group Structures and Their Functions: Kin, Neighbors and Friends." *American Sociological Review* 34 (1969): 465–81.

Lukas, J. Anthony. *Common Ground*. Knopf, 1985.

McClenahan, B. *The Changing Urban Neighborhood*. Los Angeles: University of Southern California Press, 1929.

Mannheim, Karl. *Ideology and Utopia*. New York: Harcourt Brace, 1964.

Nisbet, Robert. *Community and Power*. Oxford University Press, 1962.

Olson, Philip. "Urban Neighborhood Research: Its Development and Current Focus." *Urban Affairs Quarterly* 17 (1982): 491–528.

Park, Robert and Ernest Burgess. *The City*. Chicago: University of Chicago Press, 1925.

Powell, A., ed. *The City: Attacking Modern Myths*. Toronto: McClelland and Stewart, 1972.

Pratt, E. E. *Industrial Causes of Congestion of Population in New York City*. New York: Macmillan, 1911.

Sale, Kirkpatrick. *Human Scale*. Perigree Books, 1980.

Silverman, Carol. "Neighboring and Urbanism: Commonality Versus Friendship." *Urban Affairs Quarterly* 22 (1987): 312–28.

Slovak, Jeffrey S. "Attachments in the Nested Community: Evidence from a Case Study." *Urban Affairs Quarterly* 21 (?): 575–97.

Stein, Maurice. *The Eclipse of Community*. Princeton: Princeton University Press, 1960.

Suttles, Gerald. *Social Order of the Slum*. Chicago: University of Chicago Press, 1968.

Tilly, Charles. *From Mobilization to Revolution*. Addison-Wesley, 1978.

Tönnies, Ferdinand (1887). *Community and Society*. Translated and edited by Charles P. Loomis. The Michigan State University Press, 1957.

Tsai Y. and L. Sigelman. "The Community Question." *British Journal of Sociology* 33 (1982): 578–88.

Vidich, Arthur J. and Joseph Bensman. *Small Town in Mass Society*. Princeton: Princeton University Press, 1958.

Wellman, B. "The Community Question: The Intimate Networks of East Yorkers." *American Journal of Sociology* 84 (1979): 1201–31.

Wellman, Barry and Barry Leighton. "Networks, Neighborhoods, and Communities: Approaches to the Study of the Community Question." *Urban Affairs Quarterly* 14 (1979): 363–90.

Whyte, William H. *The Organization Man*. New York: Doubleday, 1956.

Wirth, Louis. "Urbanism as a Way of Life." *American Journal of Sociology* 44 (1938): 3–24.

Woolston, H. *A Study of the Population of Manhattanville*. New York: Macmillan, 1909.

Woolston, H. *Metropolis: A Study of Urban Communities*. Englewood Cliffs, NJ: Prentice Hall, 1938.

Zito, J. "Anonymity and Neighboring in an Urban High-Rise Complex." *Urban Life and Culture* 3 (1974): 243–63.

Index

Acquaintances, 62–66, 75–109, 129, 133
Activities, 41–57, 66–70, 129–131, 135
    Camping, 51–52
    Competing, 52
    Cooking, 53
    Dining, 51–52, 68–69
    Drinking, 51–52, 68
    Fairs, 69
    Fishing, 52
    Fish fry, 67
    Halloween party, 49–50
    Individual, 68–69
    Jogging, 54
    Picnic, 50, 67
    Reading, 54
    Relaxing, 53–54, 56, 68, 72, 130–131, 136
    Service, 66–67
    Shopping, 51, 56, 68–69
    Spectating, 52, 69
    Sports, 52, 67–68
    Traveling, 52
    Yard work, 53–54, 56, 68, 88
Age, 13–15, 37–38, 60
Atmosphere, 42–45, 60
Auction, 55–56, 63
Automobiles, 43, 64, 131
    Junked, 6, 8, 115
    Tinkering, 44–45, 48–49, 68
Autonomy, 9, 29
Banfield, Harold, 22, 147
Becker, Carl, 133
Bensman, Joseph, 5, 22, 29, 41, 149
Birch, David L., 26, 147
Beach house, 122–123
Boosters, 12, 135
Borrowing, 47, 64–65
Bott, Elizabeth, 22, 147
Bulldozing, 115
Burgess, Ernest, 24, 28, 30, 136, 148

Caplan, Gerald, 22, 147
Change, 10–12, 29, 30, 43, 122–123, 135, 137
    Perceptions, 112–115, 117–119, 124–126, 134
    Perception of decline, 44, 124, 136
    Perceptions of improvement, 44–45, 124
Charm, 3, 7, 12, 35, 42, 60, 118, 129, 135, 137–138
Chicken soup, 47, 55, 130, 137
Children, 29, 46–50, 52, 54, 61–62, 64, 70, 114, 124
Churches, 9, 53, 56, 67, 100–101
City at the gates, 115–117, 126
Civil status, 13–15
Class, 6, 10, 13–15, 37, 59–60, 137
    See grammar
Cliques, 60–62
Community, 1, 9, 12, 127
    Activities, 49–50
    Choosing Millfield for, 34–36
    Image, 41–57
    Of limited liability, 21–24, 64–65, 135
    Perceptions, 5–7, 10–12, 33–40, 73, 112–113, 129, 131
    Resources, 28–30
    Size, 42
    Studies, 19–31
    Urban, 19–21
    Conflict, 11
Corner cabinet, 35, 129
Cornfields, 7, 44, 115, 137–138
Demography, 13–15, 16–17, 114
Death, 114
Disasters, 49, 63, 116
Divorce, 12, 135
Driveways, 48
Ducks, 8, 115, 128, 138

Durkheim, Emile, 1
Economy, 9, 51, 121, 124
Education, 13–15, 37–38, 81, 103, 105, 117–123, 125, 129, 133
Effrat, Marcia, 20, 147
Elderly, 60–61
Emigration, 116–117
Everybody knows everybody, 7, 19, 35, 46, 63, 108, 127
Families, 7, 12, 13–15, 22, 29, 34, 36, 41, 59–75, 131–132, 135
    Choosing Millfield for, 34–36
    Kin, 70–72, 74, 130, 134
    Nuclear, 69–70, 132
    Socializing, 48, 52, 71–72, 130, 132
Farms, 3, 9
Feagin, J. R., 29, 147
Fears, 11, 111–126, 134
Findings, 73–74, 134–137
Firey, Walter I., 26, 147
Fischer, Claude S., 24–25, 27, 147
Flanagan, William G., 20, 147
Foley, Donald, 23, 147
Friday, 12, 51–52
Friends, 7, 75–80, 103, 105–108
    Friendliness, 7, 50, 60, 128, 137–138
    Friendships, 25, 105–108, 133
Future, 10–12, 114, 134
Galaster, George, 26, 147
Gans, Herbert J., 5, 22, 29, 147
Gemeinschaft und Gessellschaft, 20–21, 127
Gender, 12–15, 38, 135
Gentrification, 6, 33
Golf, 9, 52, 130
Good old days, 124
Grammar, 13–15, 18, 37–38, 81, 129
Grocery store, 122
Guest, A.M., 23, 147
Gusfield, J. R., 22, 147

Hall, Edward G., 17, 147
Halloween, 42, 49
Hannertz, Ulf, 24, 30, 147
Haven, 10, 42
Helping, 8, 46–47, 55, 63–64, 66, 124, 130
    Lending, 47, 53, 64–65
    Watching, 47, 54, 64–65
Heterogeneity, 60, 63
History, 10–12, 27, 43, 113, 119–123
Historical Society, 27, 43, 50, 61–62, 68, 73, 114, 118, 122, 134 128, 131
Homogeneity, 43, 63
Hoods, 61
Houses, 2, 8–9, 26, 34, 62–63, 111, 115, 123
    Choosing, 34–36
    Clapboard, 7, 115
    Cost, 33, 35
    Improving, 8, 35, 44, 53, 55, 68–69, 117–118, 124, 130–131, 136
    Ownership, 13–15, 16, 128, 135
    Ranch, 115, 118, 138
    Visiting, 46, 64
    Watching, 47
    See maps of village
Households, 13–15, 16, 77–78, 80, 83–86, 91–94, 132
Hunter, Albert, 23, 25, 147
Hypotheses, 1, 6, 10, 12, 34, 56–57, 112–113, 124–126, 134–136
Images, 6–10, 129–131
    Beehive, 128
    Chicken soup, 6–10, 47, 55, 129–131, 137
    Cornfields, 6–10, 44, 115, 129–131, 137–38
    Everybody knows everybody, 6–10, 19, 35, 46, 108, 127, 129–131
    Hasn't changed a lick, 113
    Launching pad, 6–10, 41, 127, 129–131
    Meeting at the post office, 6–10, 129–131

One big neighborhood, 62–66
Pushing the lead ball, 63
Sledding for the mail, 48, 119
Walnuts, 49
Immigrants, 5–6, 12, 128, 134
Choosing Millfield, 34–38, 135
Incorporation, 11, 113, 115–116
Individualism, 6
Interviews, 1, 13–15
Isolates, 99–101
Janowitz, Morris, 21, 23, 25, 27, 148
Jones, T. J., 22, 148
Kasarda, John, 23, 25, 27, 148
Killilea, Marie, 22, 147
Kin litanies, 71, 74
Landmarks, 28
Launching pad, 41, 127, 130
Lee, B. A., 23, 147
Leighton, Barry, 25, 28, 149
Litwak, 25, 148
Location, 81, 83, 135
Lukas, J. Anthony, 26, 28, 148
McClenahan, B., 25, 148
Mail delivery, 11, 44, 113, 119
Malls, 115
Mannheim, Karl, 23, 148
Maps
    Looking at, 65, 75
    Of village, 4, 76, 82, 84, 90–99, 102, 106
Marital status, see civil status
Meeting places, 48–49, 54–55, 61, 63, 136
Memberships, 66–68
Memories, 12, 111–126. 135
Mill, 121–123
Mosquitoes, 45
Movies, 56
Music, 48
Nature, 8, 45
Neighbors, 8, 24–27, 31, 35, 45–49, 54–56, 59–80, 131–132, 135–137

Neighborhoods, 19–31, 59, 62–66, 79–109, 114, 128–129, 131–133, 137
    Adjacency, 86–87
    Boundaries, 27–29, 60–61
    Neighborhood's neighborhoods, 95–98, 101–103
Nighdwellers, 26, 135
Nisbet, Robert, 22, 148
Nostalgia, 5
Nuclear disaster, 116
Olson, Philip, 22, 24–26, 28–29, 31, 137, 148
Park, Robert, 1, 23–24, 28, 30, 136, 148
Peace, see tranquility
Picnic, 50
Play, 9, 52
Politics, 116
Porches, 7, 46, 64
Post office 7, 9, 30, 34, 46, 48, 54, 59, 63, 80, 87–88, 113–114, 119, 127, 130–133, 135
Powell, A., 22, 19, 148
Pratt, E. E., 22, 148
Privacy, 45, 60, 128, 130, 137
Proximity, 65–66, 83–88, 108, 132, 135
Race, 37, 43, 118–119
Research method, 1–2, 16–18
Residence, length of, 13–15, 25–26, 30, 103–105, 120–121, 125 126, 128–129, 133, 135
    See demography
Residential clusters, 7, 20
Restoration, 112–113
Rituals, 24–25, 30
Safety, 8, 35, 42–43, 63–64, 128, 130
Sale, Kirkpatrick, 27, 148
Saturday, 9, 12, 22, 41–42, 52–53, 127–138
Schools, 9, 13–15, 123
Service organizations, 66–67

Setting, 2–3, 34, 36
Shils, Edward, 31, 136–137
Shopping, 51–52
Sidewalks, 11, 44, 113, 119
Sigelman, L., 27, 149
Silverman, Carol, 25–27, 75, 103, 105, 148
Slaughterhouse, 123
Slovak, Jeffrey S., 26, 148
Social interaction, 59–74
Social networks, 12, 25, 88–90, 103, 133–134, 136
Socializing, 46, 48–49, 51–52, 62–66
Sociologists, 53, 131, 138
Spouses, 9–10, 69–70
Stability, 128, 135
Stein, Maurice, 21, 148
Strangers, 8, 43, 55, 64, 128, 130
Street lights, 11, 44, 113, 119
Suburbs, 2–3, 111–112
Suttles, Gerald, 22, 148
Szelenyi, J., 25, 148
Tasi, Y., 27, 147
Taxes, 118, 128
Tilly, Charles, 29, 149
Tonnies, Ferdinand, 1, 20–22, 149
Traffic, 115, 124
Trains, 45, 49, 62–63, 121–122, 124
Tranquility, 45, 54, 127, 137–38
Trolley, 122
Trust, 8, 64, 130
Types, 59–60
Trysting places, 122
Underwear, Black, 55, 65
Uneasiness, 117–119
Urban expansion, 2
Vandalism, 61–62, 114
Vidich, Arthur J., 5, 22, 29, 41, 149
Villagers, 5
    Native, 6, 112–113, 136
    Urban, 5–6, 22–24, 41–42, 112–113, 117–118, 128, 136
Villages, 111
Walking, 7, 46, 49, 54, 63, 127, 131–133
Water, 116, 119
Weber, Max, 1
Wellman, B., 25, 28–29, 149
Whyte, William H., 27, 149
Wirth, Louis, 21, 24, 149
Woolston, H. A., 22, 149
Work, 9, 12, 13–15, 51–52, 55–56, 112
Yards, 48, 53
Zito, J., 26, 149